TEACHING Mindfulness

A GUIDEBOOK FOR TEACHERS, PARENTS, COUNSELORS, AND CAREGIVERS

We chose to print this title on responsibly harvested paper stock cer-tified by the Forest Stewardship Council®, an independent auditor of responsible forestry practices. For more information, visit us.fsc.org.

MIX
Paper from
responsible sources
FSC® C001701

© 2022 by Amoneeta Beckstein

Cover and interior design: John Wincek, aerocraftart.com
Illustrations: Alex Grey and Katherine Grace, bluehippopress.com

Printed in China

BPC
PO Box 99
Summertown, TN 38483
888-260-8458
bookpubco.com

ISBN: 978-1-939053-41-1

27 26 25 24 23 22   1 2 3 4 5 6 7 8 9

Disclaimer: The information in this book is presented for educational purposes only.

TEACHING Mindfulness

A GUIDEBOOK FOR TEACHERS, PARENTS, COUNSELORS, AND CAREGIVERS

Amoneeta Beckstein, PhD

WITH SPECIAL CONTRIBUTIONS BY

Jana York, MS

BOOK PUBLISHING COMPANY
Summertown, Tennessee

This guidebook is designed for teachers, parents, counselors, and care-givers to teach mindfulness to young children (ages 5–11) in simple and easy ways.

The curriculum includes the following:

- Background on mindfulness supported by current empirically based literature
- Comprehensive lesson plans for 5- to 11-year-olds that can be adapted for younger children or teens
- More than 40 activities written in an easy-to-understand format
- Meditation scripts to cultivate awareness of the breath, loving-kindness, body scans, and more

NOTE: The training and activities in this guidebook are secular and not intended to promote any spiritual or religious beliefs.

Contents

LESSON 3

is for Investigate

Exploring the physical sensations in the body and what they are trying to tell you

LESSON 4

O *is for* Observe 41

Noticing your thoughts, feelings, and emotions and how to respond to them

LESSON 5

U *is for* Understand 55

Learning how to be kind to yourself and others with compassion and gratitude

L E S S O N   6

Y *is for* You

Finding fun ways to use mindfulness every day

A P P E N D I X

Extra Activities

Final Notes

Preface

Teaching Mindfulness introduces a simple method that you can use to help students experience the benefits of mindfulness, including learning to be present and to focus; noticing and responding to distractions, feelings, and sensations; and increasing gratitude. It is designed for students in primary grades, ages 5–11, and can be adapted to lower, middle, and high school levels.

The purpose of the guidebook is to help you—whether you're an educator, parent, counselor, or caregiver—implement mindfulness in a variety of learning environments, including the classroom and home, using simple activities. Most activities can be adapted to distance-learning formats too.

You may well have *wanted* to introduce mindfulness to students in the past but, due to time constraints, thought you couldn't fit it into your schedule. Yet you may be surprised to discover that you've already been practicing and teaching some mindfulness without realizing it, and can regularly and easily slip in more during small blocks of free time.

Our intention is for this program to serve as a preventative tool by helping young children cope with emotional issues in today's complex and fast-paced society. At the same time, we hope to help adults who work with children manage their own increasing levels of stress by engaging in mindfulness and becoming more mindful themselves.

We believe it is imperative that educators have a foundation of self-care and compassion to help cultivate awareness of mindfulness practices in young children. To that end, as we developed this curriculum, we carefully considered teachers' and administrators' time constraints and the challenges they face when implementing new programs in their school systems. Our goal was to create a curriculum so simple that any teacher, counselor, parent, or caregiver can deliver it with confidence and ease.

As part of the development of this guidebook, we also immersed ourselves in research focused on adverse childhood experiences (ACE) and children's need for social-emotional learning (SEL). For the past nine years we've introduced mindfulness to communities around the globe, teaching introductory sessions to adults, establishing an eight-week mindfulness-based stress reduction program, and helping to implement mindfulness programs in schools. Along the way, we've collected positive objective and subjective data as well as testimonials that have confirmed what we've long known: we all can benefit from mindfulness for anxiety relief, self-regulation, compassion, and thriving in this busy world.

Introduction

Why Do Children Need Mindfulness?

When you were in elementary school and the teacher called your name for roll, you most likely answered, "PRESENT!" (or "Here!"). The question is, were you really?

In schools today, a lot of time is spent on academics and developing creativity through art, music, and expression. Students are taught how to strengthen their bodies through exercise and sports. However, it seems less attention is given to the fundamental functions of their minds. When students discover mindfulness, however, they develop an innate capacity to use their minds with more attention and awareness, which can lead to more success in the above-mentioned areas and much more.

THE MANY BENEFITS OF MINDFULNESS

Mindfulness not only is associated with physical health benefits (Murphy et al. 2012), but also has been shown to help students regulate emotions, improve focus, become more relaxed and calm, and feel more creative and confident (Bochun 2011; Meiklejohn et al. 2012; Napoli, Krech, and Holley 2005; Zelazo and Lyons 2012). Other benefits include improved social skills, self-awareness, memory, mood, and other mental health indices, such as reduced stress and anxiety (Meiklejohn).

However, mindfulness is much more than all that even! It is about guiding children to learn how to self-regulate, helping them understand the power of choice, and providing them with resources and encouragement. Some students trained in mindfulness have been shown to use it to cope with uncomfortable emotions and improve their emotional well-being (Viafora, Mathiesen, and Unsworth 2014). New research suggests that self-regulation (a child's ability to manage thoughts, behaviors, and emotions) is the biggest predictor of success; in fact, it can influence lifelong "achievement, interpersonal behaviors, mental health, and healthy living" (Robson, Allen, and Howard 2020, 324). Essentially, through mindfulness training, we are planting seeds to help children grow more resilient.

It's not just students who benefit from using mindfulness: teachers also experience advantages, such as greater "well-being and teaching self-efficacy, as well as their ability to manage classroom behavior and establish and maintain supportive relationships with students" (Meiklejohn et al. 2012, 291). Furthermore, mindfulness appears to boost students' engagement and perception of the school climate, likely making teachers' work easier. Moreover, there is mounting scientific evidence that "mindfulness for young people is easy to carry out, fits into a wide range of contexts, is enjoyed by both students and teachers, and does no harm" (Weare 2012, 2).

Thus, integrating mindfulness into school curricula is likely to have both personal and academic advantages for both teachers and students (Leland 2015; Meiklejohn et al. 2012). Many schools in Asia—including most schools in Thailand—have realized this and integrated mindfulness curriculum throughout their schools (Klechaya and Glasson 2017). Some US educators have also started implementing it in their schools (Mindful Schools 2010–2019).

Mindfulness seems to be gaining in popularity and relevance in every culture. Mindful Schools claims that there are mindfulness teachers in over 100 countries, reaching "more than 3 million children" globally. And that is precisely why we've developed this book: to give teachers everywhere empirically based exercises for integrating mindfulness into their classrooms and discussion questions for enhancing critical thinking skills.

HOW TO USE THIS GUIDEBOOK

Now that we have established the importance of teaching mindfulness to young children, let us introduce you to our curriculum of themed lesson plans that we call the *vowels of mindfulness* based on the English-language vowels.

The vowels are used as a mnemonic device, with each vowel representing a lesson that helps students develop present-moment awareness: Attention, Experience, Investigate, Observe, and Understand. A bonus lesson (**Y** is for You) is designed to show students how to incorporate the previous lessons into their daily lives.

A stands for Attention and it aims to bring you into the present moment by being still, learning to focus, and paying attention to what is happening now.

E stands for Experience and it aims to help you enjoy the present moment using all five senses: taste, touch, sight, smell, and hearing. You can practice shifting from the go-to "thinking" mode into the less-frequently used "sensing" mode.

I stands for Investigate and it aims to help you explore the physical sensations in the body and what they are trying to tell you. Learn to be curious about what is happening in your body without judgment.

O stands for Observe and it aims to help you notice and respond to your thoughts, feelings, and emotions, and to stay curious about what is happening in your mind while suspending judgment. Experience ways to create space between thought and action.

U stands for Understand and it aims to help you practice being kind to yourself and others with both compassion and gratitude. Practice bringing a smile to yourself—and others.

Y stands for You and it aims to help you find fun ways to use mindfulness every day. The lifelong journey of weaving mindfulness into your daily life begins here.

The eight-week program is designed for you to set aside 15 minutes for each themed lesson, once or twice a week, and repeat mindfulness practices throughout the day, as time allows. We encourage you to implement as much or as little of the program as you'd like, and even delve deeper if desired.

Each 15-minute lesson contains pedagogical classroom material, such as objectives, background, lesson planning and rationale, and relevant activities. The goal for each activity is to provide young children with fun and interactive ways to learn skills, tools, and techniques to help with self-regulation and a growth mindset while building resilience and self-confidence.

In addition to the lesson plans and activities, throughout the guidebook you'll find suggested scripts, examples, encouragement, guidance, and our own personal reflections. The purpose of the guide is to support you while you engage children in the key components of the mindfulness curriculum.

is for Attention

Learn how to focus and pay attention to what is happening now

OBJECTIVES

1. Introduce and define mindfulness.
2. Learn how to pay attention and what it means (feels, looks like) to pay attention.
3. Demonstrate ways to pay attention: posture, breathing, anchor words.
4. Explore anchor words such as *calm*, *relax*, and *breathe*.

THE VOWELS OF MINDFULNESS

"Mindfulness is paying attention on purpose in the present moment with kindness and curiosity."

JON KABAT-ZINN

MINDFUL BODIES ··········   ANCHOR WORDS CALM RELAX BREATHE ··········   FOCUS ON YOUR BREATH

ACTIVITY: Mindful bodies, awareness of breathing, anchor words. Practice mindful breathing for one minute.

A is for Attention

Focus or concentrate on what is happening now.
While it is important to pay attention to many things,
you can also use mindfulness with a spirit of curiosity
and a sense of wonderment.

Introduction

What is mindfulness?

Discussion Question

"Does anyone know what *mindfulness* is? What does the word mean?"

Quote

Jon Kabat-Zinn, known as the father of mindfulness, defines mindfulness as "paying attention in a particular way: on purpose in the present moment and non-judgmentally" (1994, 4).

Teacher's Answer

Mindfulness is paying attention to the present moment without judgment (Kabat-Zinn 1994). This usually means without thought. When you are listening, really listen: don't label; don't judge. When you are eating, use your sense of taste; don't think about what you eat. Most of us spend up to 50 percent of the day with a wandering mind, and sometimes we live a bit too much in our thoughts. Those thoughts are quite often negative, judgmental, and not very helpful. Negativity can look like criticism of yourself and others or can be in the form of fear, which quite often prevents you from living your best and happiest life. We'll talk about this more in another lesson, but for now, we are really wanting to understand what mindfulness is and how it can help you.

A is for Attention

Ask students to think about and try to remember their own experience when they heard the statement "PAY ATTENTION!" Write this on the board in all CAPS and explain that often the words are said loudly by a parent, teacher, coach, or sibling. Explain further that, while the goal is to acquire some sense of focus, a loud tone or harsh voice often creates more of an emotional stimulation or distraction.

Acknowledge that students are often told to pay attention, but then ask them, "Were you shown *how* to pay attention?" Hence the letter *A*!

Show the infographic about the attention span of human beings getting shorter over the years (see pages 96 and 97).

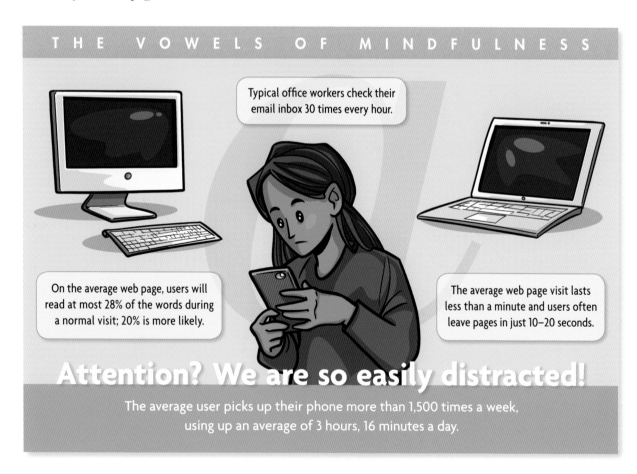

THE VOWELS OF MINDFULNESS

Typical office workers check their email inbox 30 times every hour.

On the average web page, users will read at most 28% of the words during a normal visit; 20% is more likely.

The average web page visit lasts less than a minute and users often leave pages in just 10–20 seconds.

Attention? We are so easily distracted!

The average user picks up their phone more than 1,500 times a week, using up an average of 3 hours, 16 minutes a day.

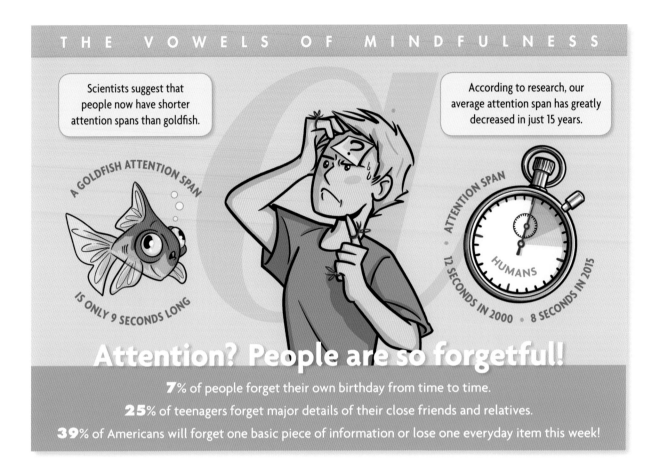

Scientists suggest that people now have shorter attention spans than goldfish.

According to research, our average attention span has greatly decreased in just 15 years.

A GOLDFISH ATTENTION SPAN IS ONLY 9 SECONDS LONG

ATTENTION SPAN · HUMANS · 12 SECONDS IN 2000 · 8 SECONDS IN 2015

Attention? People are so forgetful!

7% of people forget their own birthday from time to time.

25% of teenagers forget major details of their close friends and relatives.

39% of Americans will forget one basic piece of information or lose one everyday item this week!

"The average adult attention span in 2002 [was] 12 seconds" while the "average attention span in 2013 was 8.25 seconds." Contrast that with the attention span of a goldfish, which is 9 seconds (Wyzowl, n.d.).

Explain that humans tend to get distracted, and a lack of attention can cause some problems. Further explain that learning about awareness and attention can provide them with the tools to help them focus.

Show the students that we have a lot of distractions and trying to stay focused on the task at hand can be challenging for many reasons. You can give an example of how screen time impacts a person's ability to pay attention.

Author's Note

I usually ask my students to track their smartphone screen time for one week. This can easily be done either by downloading a free app or using a phone's tracking features. My students consistently report being surprised by how much time they spend on their phones and their high number of "pickups"—number of times they open the phone. The former is often more than 5 hours a day and the latter more than 500 times a day. This is consistent with research that shows that the majority of American 8- to 12-year-olds have smartphones and that they spend just under 5 hours a day on them (Rideout and Robb 2019).

ATTENTION: Focus or concentrate on what is happening in the *here and now*. While it is important to pay attention to many things, you can use mindfulness with a spirit of curiosity and a sense of wonderment.

Note for Teachers

The key to learning to pay attention is consistency and repetition. It is important to use the tools or techniques yourself and, with an open mind, find your own unique ways to teach your students how to learn stillness at their current level. Once understood, it serves as an excellent preparatory stage for the start of any lesson.

ACTIVITY

Spotlight

Use a "spotlight" to represent a focus point and show what attention looks like.

PREPARATION: Flashlight

INSTRUCTIONS:

1. Darken the room by closing the blinds and dimming the lights.
2. Shine the flashlight around the room.
3. Explain that the moving flashlight demonstrates how attention jumps from one thing to another.
4. Next, shine the flashlight on one object for a longer duration.
5. Explain that attention becomes very still and calm when it is focused on one object. A focused mind is the opposite of a distracted mind, sometimes called "monkey mind" because it jumps from place to place.

ACTIVITY

Telescope Eyes

PREPARATION: Ask students to bring tubes from home: a cardboard paper towel roll or even a rolled-up piece of paper will do.

INSTRUCTIONS: Explain that students can use their tubes like a telescope, which is an instrument that makes distant objects appear magnified. Students can enhance their "attention lens" by focusing their tube on an object in the classroom or out the window.

Have the students color the rolls with markers or add decorative tape.

Mind Your Posture: Getting Set

Often called "mindful bodies" or "mindful posture," getting into a mindful position helps cultivate focused attention.

Being in a mindful posture is recommended in the pre-learning or warm-up stage. Just like an athlete needs to be in the proper stance for sports, or a musician positions their instrument in preparation to play, a person practicing mindfulness also needs to start in a proper stance. You can demonstrate the football three-point stance or bring an instrument, such as a trumpet or a flute, to your mouth.

Suggested Script

We often use the action of puppies to illustrate busy minds. We call this the "puppy mind." Puppies have a difficult time staying still and are easily distracted. It takes practice and patience to train your mind and body to be still. Have you ever noticed a dog's posture in full attention mode? Dogs will sit with a very upright and still posture as they scan the yard or survey the scene for danger or are very alert as they use their keen eyesight for the pleasure of chasing birds.

Dogs really do show us how to be mindful. They always focus their attention on the present, most love unconditionally and without judgment, and they efficiently use all their senses to gain information.

Option: Show the Mindfulness in Schools Project (MiSP) *Playing Attention* animated video (youtube.com/watch?v=LgXZW6Xqokw; 2016), which uses the illustration of how our attention is like a puppy that is all over the place and needs to be trained with patience and kindness. Pause at the one-minute mark if you sense that your students are not ready for a full nine minutes of stillness and mindfulness practice.

Note for Teachers

Whether or not your school has a pet therapy program, you may want to speak with your administration about inviting a dog handler and pet to class so students can observe and benefit from their affectionate and mindful behavior firsthand.

Mindful Posture

To achieve the desired mindful posture, students will need to be as still as they can. Ask them to sit and direct their attention toward you. Acknowledge that it is okay to scratch an itch, or readjust themselves or their clothes to be comfortable and alert. Observe each student's posture; some will be too rigid, so encourage them to relax.

INSTRUCTIONS:

1. Explain that they're about to learn how to put on their "mindful bodies."
2. Instruct students to sit upright but not too rigid—tall like a tree or like a still dog.
3. Have them put their hands in their lap or on their desk.
4. Encourage them to relax their shoulders and place their feet flat on the floor.
5. Once ready, invite students to lower their gaze or close their eyes if that is comfortable.
6. When teaching the mindful posture, keep the practice very brief at first and increase the time as students get accustomed to being still.

ACTIVITY OPTION

Mindful Posture with Bell

PREPARATION: Small chime or bell

INSTRUCTIONS:

1. Follow the Mindful Posture instructions above. Signal the end of the practice by telling students you will ring the bell and ask them to listen until it fades away.
2. Say, "Once you no longer hear the bell, quietly raise your hand or open your eyes."
3. You can also ask them to open their eyes and smile when they no longer hear the sound.

Who doesn't want to see a class of smiling faces? This is just an introduction. There is more about being mindful of sounds in Lesson 2, *E is for Experience*.

Remember to carefully consider *how* you use the bell in your classroom. The bell serves as a cue to prepare for something, right? It can become more of a distraction if not used properly.

Contributor's Note

I once visited a middle school classroom to teach an eight-week mindfulness curriculum, and upon entry, the teacher rang the bell incessantly while giving loud instructions to quiet down and pay attention. Although I appreciated the teacher's effort to maintain order, it was clear that the students were ignoring the bell, so chaos ensued. It was like the bell was a signal to go crazy. (Tweens!) Fortunately, I was able to gradually gather their attention by asking what the bell meant to them and discussing how we could use it best to meet our goals collectively. We talked about the bell serving as a check-in point for where they were at the present moment. We went around the room and students gave single-word descriptions of how they were feeling before we started the practice (example responses: happy, tired, anxious). Also, I allowed students to lead the exercise by taking turns ringing the bell. I guess you could say I met them where they currently were.

ACTIVITY

Focus on Your Breath

The purpose of teaching about the breath is to give students something to direct their focus on in the present moment. Noticing your breathing helps calm your body as well (Sessa 2007). The breath will become a vital part of each practice and unfold as a tool for self-regulation.

INSTRUCTIONS:

1. Demonstrate a deep breath. Ask students to take a deep breath, repeat, and then just breathe normally.
2. Invite them to examine their breath a little closer by asking them to place one hand on their belly and breathe normally with slow, quiet breaths.
3. Ask them to notice what happens to the belly when they breathe.
4. Now, ask them to try placing their hand on their chest for a few breaths.
5. Next, ask them to think of their breath as a balloon filling with air. You can also use a breathing ball (also known as the Hoberman Sphere) to illustrate (Willard and Nance 2018).
6. Last of all, draw their attention to the breath by asking, "Does the balloon inflate with the in breath or the out breath?"

TEACHER'S TIP: An easy way to remember: an "in" breath *in*flates the belly.

ACTIVITY

Belly Breathing Buddies

This activity is a great way to start the day and is common in schools that have mindfulness programs. It works great for younger students and those new to learning to focus on the breath.

PREPARATION: You will need enough space for students to lie down on the carpet or floor, as well as stuffed toys, small rocks, or other lightweight objects.

INSTRUCTIONS:

1. Review the breathing exercises from the Focus on Your Breath activity (see page 8).

2. Have each student place a stuffed toy or other lightweight object on their belly. Ask them to start to inhale slowly, fill up their bellies with air, and slowly breathe out through the mouth or nose as they exhale.

3. Allow them to do this on their own and notice how their body feels.

ACTIVITY OPTION

Imaginative Belly Breathing Buddies

Encourage students to use their imagination by giving names to the breath.

ALLIGATOR BREATH: Ask students to breathe in, with outstretched arms opening like a gator's mouth, and exhale as they bring their arms down like they're closing the gator's mouth.

HOT CHOCOLATE BREATH: Instruct students to breathe in through the nose as if they are smelling hot chocolate, and exhale as they blow out softly through the mouth like they're cooling the cup of cocoa.

ACTIVITY

My Anchor Mate

INSTRUCTIONS:

1. Explain why we use the word *anchor*: An anchor is commonly used to illustrate how the mind wanders and the anchor can bring it back to the present moment.

2. Explain why we use the word *mate*: *Mate* is a British term for *friend* or *fellow*. Your anchor can be like a friend reminding you to come back to the present moment.

3. Further explain:

   *"An anchor helps keep the boat where it is. If the boat starts to drift away, the anchor pulls it back in. Well, that is what our breathing is doing for our mind. Sometimes when you try to focus on your breath, you might find

*Excerpt reproduced with permission from *Mindful Schools* (2014, 9).

that your mind starts thinking instead of focusing on your breath. When our mind wanders away from our breath or starts to think about things, we can notice it and bring it right back to our anchor."

Note for Teachers

Many mindfulness teachings use words or short phrases to help as a focal point for the anchor. These words might include *calm*, *relax*, or *breathe*. It's helpful to bring in anchor mate words slowly and allow students to choose their own words silently. If they feel comfortable, they can then share their chosen words. It's okay if students change their anchor mates to suit how they're feeling in the present moment. If a student is feeling anxious because of a test, it might be "relax, relax, relax." If a student is feeling anxious because a sibling or bully is aggravating them, it might be "stay calm, stay calm, stay calm."

An anchor may also serve as a focal point during movement. If you are riding your bike and want to be mindful, you could notice the rotation for a moment as you pedal; if you are jogging, you could notice your feet touching the ground. If attempting to learn a song or a cheer that requires rhythm, clap your hands to the beat—"clap, clap, clap"—or practice listening to the sound as your anchor. As students become familiar with learning to focus and dealing with their own personal distractions, they will gradually find and develop their own anchor words.

ACTIVITY

Anchor Breathing

Suggested Script

To help you focus on just breathing, we can add an anchor word or a short phrase like "relax," or "just breathe." Let's use the word *relax* to start and later you can decide on what your own personal anchor word or phrase will be.

INSTRUCTIONS:

1. Have students sit up straight and comfortably.
2. Have them take a few breaths, inhaling gently through the nose and out through the mouth.
3. Now, ask them to say their anchor words silently with each out breath.
4. Acknowledge that they might notice their minds wandering and encourage them to just keep saying their anchor word or "relax" with the out breath.

In the beginning, this activity is harder than it sounds. Think of the brain as a muscle that, like any other part of the body, needs to be exercised. With practice, this is an extremely valuable tool that enhances the mind-body connection.

More information on this will be offered later with the Count to 10 activity in Lesson 4 (see page 53).

Watch the one-minute *Breathing Anchor* YouTube video created by Hopkins Education Services (youtube.com/watch?v=yZYUJafIKOs; Hopkins 2016).

(see page 53)

ACTIVITY

Pass the Cup

Pass the Cup was created by Susan Kaiser Greenland (2016). This activity is growing in popularity at adult workshops and conferences because participants say it helps them feel more focused, caring, and connected. Not to mention—it's fun! Here is what Greenland says:

> Pass the Cup is a playful way for young children to build concentration and develop awareness of how their bodies move through space. While encouraging teamwork and coordination, Pass the Cup also builds young children's awareness of their bodies as they relate to other people (arms, legs, hands, elbows) and things (tables, chairs, cups of water), as well as awareness of the quality of their movements (sluggish, quick, fluid, jerky). To prepare, fill a small unbreakable cup with water to about one inch from the rim. Using teamwork and paying attention to what's happening around us, we pass the cup filled with water without spilling a drop. First, we pass it with our eyes open and then with our eyes closed.

PREPARATION: Fill a metal cup almost to the top with water.

INSTRUCTIONS:

1. Say, "We're going to pass this cup to one another without spilling any water. What do we have to pay attention to so that the water does not spill?" (Example responses: looking at the cup and one another, feeling with our hands, moving our arms slowly.)

2. Now say, "Are you ready? Let's try it." Help children silently pass the cup of water back and forth between them two or three times (or around the circle).

3. Tell the students, "Now let's see if we can pass the cup with our eyes and mouths closed. What types of things will we need to pay attention to if we can't talk or see?" (Example responses: the sound of clothing rustling, the feeling of the person sitting next to us moving, the feeling of the cup in our hands.) Help children silently pass the cup with their eyes closed.

TEACHER'S TIPS:

1. If playing with very young children, first practice by passing a closed water bottle. When children are ready, graduate to passing an open cup.

2. Fill the cup high enough that it is challenging for children to not spill the water but not too high that they cannot be successful at the game.

3. If playing with a group, sit in a circle. After the first round, pass the cup in the opposite direction. In the next set of activities, children apply the life skills and themes that they have learned through introspective games to their conversations with friends and family.

NOTE: We encourage using a metal cup to protect the environment (say no to plastic), and it seems to add more to the sense of touch because of the cool temperature and moisture beading on the metal.

Critical Thinking!

Discuss with the students how they can use this *A* vowel to help themselves at school, home, or play. Where is their attention right now? What are their anchors of attention?

Challenge

- Practice deep breathing for 30 seconds and then increase the time to 1 minute.
- Allow a student to lead the Mindful Posture (see page 6) and Focus on Your Breath (see page 8) awareness activities. Use a bell and timer for added fun.

is for Experience

Enjoy the present moment using your senses of sight, sound, touch, taste, and smell

OBJECTIVES

1. Explore a variety of ways to use your senses (sight, sound, touch, taste, smell) to be in the present moment.
2. Learn how to focus with one-pointed attention.
3. Define intention versus goals.
4. Develop bite-sized attention and appreciation for what is here and now.

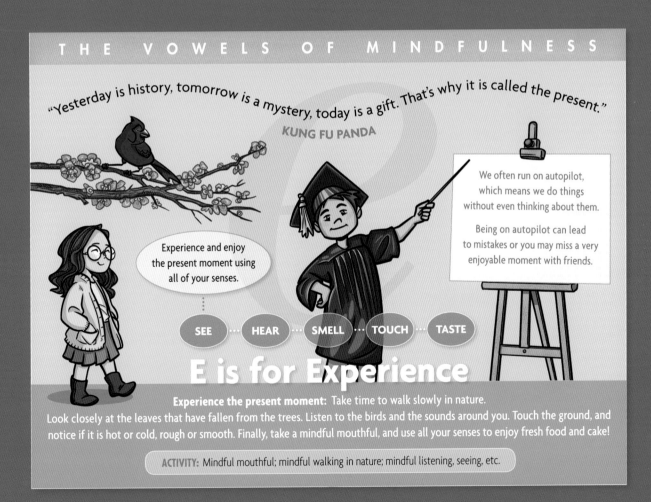

THE VOWELS OF MINDFULNESS

"Yesterday is history, tomorrow is a mystery, today is a gift. That's why it is called the present."

KUNG FU PANDA

Experience and enjoy the present moment using all of your senses.

We often run on autopilot, which means we do things without even thinking about them.

Being on autopilot can lead to mistakes or you may miss a very enjoyable moment with friends.

SEE ··· HEAR ··· SMELL ··· TOUCH ··· TASTE

E is for Experience

Experience the present moment: Take time to walk slowly in nature.
Look closely at the leaves that have fallen from the trees. Listen to the birds and the sounds around you. Touch the ground, and notice if it is hot or cold, rough or smooth. Finally, take a mindful mouthful, and use all your senses to enjoy fresh food and cake!

ACTIVITY: Mindful mouthful; mindful walking in nature; mindful listening, seeing, etc.

Introduction

This is an action-packed lesson with a lot of sensing and fun activities to try! You can integrate these activities into the standard curriculum by adding them to current core-subject lesson plans. For example, if students are learning about nutrition, you might introduce the Mindful Eating activity (see page 20). Lessons can easily be linked to other aspects of the curriculum in many other subjects.

Depending upon the ages of your students, you may want to start by introducing key words and concepts—such as *autopilot*, *intention*, and *goal*. Of course, use your discretion: you know your students best. (Remember, this is just a guide.)

AUTOPILOT

Discussion Question

First, ask the students what they think an *autopilot* is, and how they think this term is linked to mindfulness.

Teacher's Answer

Autopilot is defined as a device that automatically maintains an aircraft on a preset course.

To do something on autopilot means to do it without conscious thought or focusing on it. We often run on autopilot, which means we do things without even thinking about them. Being on autopilot can lead to costly mistakes (Hyman 2014) or missing a very enjoyable moment with friends.

INTENTION

Instead, allowing yourself to experience a moment with *intention* can make an ordinary task extraordinary! Understanding the difference between goals and intentions may help students tune in to the moment more purposely.

An *intention* is an aim or plan. Something that you decide to do with purpose. If you are going to set an intention, you could ask yourself, "What is it I would like to happen now?"

GOAL

A *goal* is a destination for a specific achievement. Goals are focused on the future, while intentions are more related to the present moment.

Here's an example to illustrate the difference between an intention and a goal. Say you are going to climb a mountain. Your goal is to reach the top. Your intention is to notice the terrain, the sounds in the forest, the smell in the air, any tastes in your mouth, and the sensation of your breath while making your way up the mountain.

Discussion Question

Which of the following statements is an example of an intention and which is an example of being on autopilot?

- I took time to walk slowly in nature to notice the leaves and trees.
- I walk to school three times a week.
- I went outside to smell the fresh grass after someone mowed the lawn.
- I hear birds on the way home from school every day.
- I listened to the birds and noticed the variety of sounds they make.
- I ate my lunch in five minutes.
- I took a mindful mouthful and used all my senses to enjoy a slice of cake.

E is for Experience

Being Present

We spend a lot of the time in the past and in the future but we rarely live in the moment.

Quote

"Yesterday is history, tomorrow is a mystery, today is a gift. That is why it's called the present." —Master Oogway, *Kung Fu Panda*

Write the quote on the board and ask the students if they have ever heard it before, and where. Discuss the meaning. (Hint: it is from a movie and a turtle says it.)

Watch the two-minute *Kung Fu Panda: Today Is a Gift* video (youtube.com/watch?v=H7BwWNMFJwE; Ideas2earnmore 2011).

EXPERIENCE: Use your senses to experience the world: see it, listen to it, touch it, taste it, and smell it.

ACTIVITY

Mindful Seeing

Tell the students that the purpose of this activity is to see something they always see but with more focus and attention. Suggest that they look at the object as if it were the first time in their life they ever saw it, and then try to describe it in their mind (example responses: shiny, smooth, bright, dull, round, flat) as they are observing it.

INSTRUCTIONS:

1. Say to the students, "Mindful posture, please."
2. Tell them to take a quick look around the room and find an object.
3. Give the students about 10 seconds to find their object.
4. Have them observe the object for about 60 seconds.
5. Divide students into small groups or pairs and allow them to share what they observed with their eyes.
6. Debrief together as a class. Ask, "Did your mind wander as you were seeing your object?" "Did the object remind you of something else, or a memory, or something you will do in the future?"

ACTIVITY OPTION

Mindful Seeing

Ask students to take a few moments to look around the room and notice something they have not seen before. These can be shapes, colors, or movements. Allow them to share. You can also add something new to the room or shift an object's location.

Remind them that when they use their mindful eyes, they can see something new or different. Mindful seeing also can help you to calm down and focus on the present.

Challenge

Invite students to take a few minutes every day to pause and observe something (objects in nature, a pencil, a shoe, a cup of water, or raindrops on a window-pane are just a few examples). Ask them to try not to decide if it is likable or unlikable; rather, describe what it looks like without emotional attachment.

Mindfulness invites one to be curious, or just open to what is happening right now. We often refer to it as a beginner's mind (Kabat-Zinn 2016).

Contributor's Personal Reflection

When I was young, I loved to play outside and explore lots of things. Rainy days found me staring out the window, wishing away the rain. One day, as I was staring at the rain, I noticed the raindrops dripping down the windowpane. I was intrigued by the shapes of the drops, the shiny ones, cloudy ones, and the fast ones. So I created a game in my mind to try to guess which raindrop would drip down the window the fastest. It entertained me for hours or probably only 15 minutes, which seems like hours to a child. Without realizing it, I was using my mindful eyes. I was truly present in those moments, alone with the raindrops on the windowpane.

ACTIVITY

Being Mindful of Sound

Listening on purpose is a skill that children are still developing. In some cases, adults, too, are developing this skill as they practice active listening. Practicing listening to different sounds can be useful in cultivating listening skills. Listening can be used as a practice to help calm the class, or relax them while they prepare for—or complete—a specific task, like taking a test.

Below are ways you can listen intentionally to the many sounds that are always around you. There are sounds indoors, outdoors, or even inside of you (such as a rumbling stomach).

- Try listening to sounds in the lunchroom. Sounds of people talking, dishes clanging, chairs moving. Sounds you usually never really pay attention to. You might not have ever noticed the loudness before.

- Try listening to sounds on the playground. Teachers themselves may experience inner pleasure while watching their students play. There is nothing more joyful than listening to children laugh and play.

- Stop and listen to the noises as far away as possible. Listen to the noises as close to you as possible. How about inside of you?

Contributor's Note

I feel it is sometimes important to share your own experiences when teaching mindfulness. As a teacher, you tend to know when the time feels right.

For example, I might share the following with a class I am teaching: "A few days ago, I was making dinner and decided to use my mindfulness. I listened very intently to all the sounds in the kitchen. The chopping sound of cutting fresh veggies, the sound of the water boiling, and the 'ding' of the cooking timer. As I turned off the stove and all the appliances and was ready to serve the dinner, I noticed the sound of water dripping. I followed the sound intently and found that there was a small water leak under the sink. Luckily, I caught it in time and was able to have a plumber fix it before it damaged anything in the kitchen. Mindfulness really paid off."

Here is another experience I sometimes share: "Growing up, we had box fans in various rooms to keep the air circulating and cool down our house. I loved listening to the fan and felt relaxed by its sound. Sometimes, I would take my curiosity close to the fan and sing songs or speak and just listen to my voice through the 'whir' sounds. Pretty sure you have tried it, and if not, give it a go just for fun."

Once you share your story, I think you will find that students are ready to share and might have already experienced mindfulness in their everyday life without realizing it.

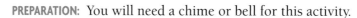

ACTIVITY

Mindful Listening

PREPARATION: You will need a chime or bell for this activity.

INSTRUCTIONS:

1. Tell the students that they are going to use their sense of hearing in this activity.
2. Ask them to sit very still with their mindful posture and take in a deep breath.
3. Explain that you will use a chime and invite them to listen to the sound.
4. Tell them to raise their hand when they can no longer hear the chime.
5. Sound the chime.
6. Do this again, but this time have them try it with their eyes closed.
7. Try this one more time, but without the chime. They will just use their ears to listen to the sounds around them.
8. Tell them that they will be listening to sounds around the room, outside of the room, and maybe even inside their body (like a rumbling stomach).
9. Try this for 60 seconds.
10. Invite students to share what sounds they heard.

Contributor's Note

Choose your words wisely. Humor and humility are musts when teaching mindfulness. I often state that I learn more from the students than I teach them. And sometimes, it is a lesson in choosing your words.

Once, I was asked to spend 15 minutes with third graders and share an activity about using your senses that was engaging and educational. I chose what I thought would be the perfect activity for the sense of sound.

"Make it rain" was a poor choice of words that turned into a mistake.

In this particular session, I was attempting to illustrate sound. "Class, did you know we can make sounds with our bodies that sound like other sounds?" Of course, in my naïve mind, I never fathomed what would ensue: the sounds of flatulence rained down in the room. "Okay," I thought, "you got me." Without telling them what sound we were going to create, I asked students to follow my instructions. I divided the class into three groups. Group one was to snap their fingers; group two was to rub their hands together lightly; group three was to gently pat their hands on their thighs.

I pointed to group one, then group two, and finally group three. I was bursting with enthusiasm as I anticipated them being able to identify the sound. To add some flair to our handmade sound bite, I blurted, "Okay, all together now, make it rain!" At once, they all started with the motion of sailing bills toward me like I was an exotic dancer. I turned three shades of red when I realized that they were making the pop culture gesture for "making it rain."

Choose your words wisely and find humor in your mindfulness journey. In the above case, despite my initial embarrassment, I can honestly say we were engaged, connected, and paying attention. This is what mindfulness is all about!

Mindful Eating

Nutrition is important to the mind and the body. Skipping meals, especially breakfast, loading up on sugary foods, and neglecting to eat vegetables can cause slower brain function, attention and mental health problems, and sluggishness among children (Giovannini et al. 2008; Hoyland, Dye, and Lawton 2009; O'Sullivan et al 2009).

By experiencing mindful eating, you can improve your alertness and be the healthiest version of yourself. Here are some tips to enjoy a MEAL mindfully:

M = MINDFUL MOUTHFUL. Try to eat slowly and fully chew your food to help with digestion. Savor at least one bite. Savoring might even boost your happiness (Carr 2011).

E = ENHANCE. Enhance your contact with food by using your senses of smell, sight, and taste. Be in the moment: when you eat, just eat!

A = AWARENESS. Be aware of your emotions. Are you stress eating or mindless snacking? Take a deep breath and check in with your feelings. Remind yourself that food is the fuel that nourishes your body.

L = LOVE. Give your food some love. Pause before you eat and offer some gratitude for what it took to bring this food from the farm to your fork.

Mindful Eating

The purpose of this activity is to invite students to see an object (do not tell them what it is) like they are aliens or as if they have never seen this object before (similar to the Mindful Seeing activity; see page 16). Students love this exercise!

PREPARATION:

1. You will need enough raisins, pieces of chocolate (Hershey's Kisses work well), foil, and cupcake liners for each student. (Make sure in advance that no students have allergies to the edible objects.)

2. Wrap the raisins or chocolate in the foil and place them in individual cupcake liners.

3. Instruct students to wash their hands or use hand sanitizer for germ control.

4. Be aware that this activity can get a little rowdy, but that is okay as long as it is in control. We all get excited about food, right?

INSTRUCTIONS:

1. Tell the students that they will use all their senses for this activity: seeing, smelling, tasting, hearing, and feeling.

2. Pass out one foil-wrapped cupcake liner to each student and ask them to observe the object with their "alien eyes."

3. Allow students to slowly open the object and place it in the palm of their hand. It will instantly become obvious that it is a raisin.

4. Ask the students to look at the object and describe it in their own words without naming it (hints: crinkly, smooth, oblong).

5. Next, have them bring the raisin to their ear and roll it in their fingers. Ask, "Does it make a sound?"

6. Next, instruct them to bring it to their nose and describe the smell.

7. Ask the students if they notice anything happening in their mouth or other parts of the body (example responses: mouth watering, stomach growling).

8. Next, ask the students to place the food on their tongue, but not to chew it yet. Say, "Notice the texture on your tongue and describe it if you can."

9. Finally, allow them to slowly chew the food and even notice the sensation of swallowing in their throat.

10. Repeat the exercise with a chocolate Kiss or some other sweet treat.

TEACHER'S TIP: Much like our life experiences, our taste buds change throughout life, so consider re-tasting veggies and fruits that you possibly did not like before.

Challenge

Encourage students to eat one meal or at least one mouthful every day in a mindful manner. Suggest that they share the activity with their parents. You can even have them fill out a reflection sheet about mindful eating as homework.

ACTIVITY

Using Your Sense of Smell

This group activity cultivates awareness, focus, and calm in the classroom by having students use their sense of smell.

PREPARATION: Gather about five different scents and put them in opaque sealed jars with holes to allow the scent to be detected. Keep the scents as natural as possible, such as a blooming aromatic flower, fresh or dried herbs, citrus peels, grass clippings, or lavender oil. Add something that does not smell very pleasant, too, such as durian. We recommend using metal spice jars that have been thoroughly cleaned and are scent-free. Paper cups or cupcake liners will also do. (But avoid using plastic or glass.) You could add another dimension to this activity by asking, "Is it something natural or processed?" *Natural* in this case means it comes from the ground.

INSTRUCTIONS:

1. Divide students into small table groups. Tell them they will be working together to identify a scent.

2. At each table, assign one presenter and one recorder.

3. The presenter asks participants to take turns closing their eyes, sniffing the scent, and describing what they think it is. Each can say what it reminds them of, if anything comes to mind.

4. The recorder writes down the name of the scent and if it is natural or processed.

5. After each participant at the table has named a scent, the recorder tallies the results and gives them to the presenter. It is not important to identify

which student said which scent. Rather, the recorder gives the *collective* results. For example, the recorder might report that two people guessed the scent was roses and one guessed it was apples.

DISCUSSION: Talk about what they smelled and how that smell makes them feel or what it reminds them of. Ask, "What did you notice in the differences in the scents? Was it something sweet? Did it smell fresh or sour?"

There is a lot to experience and explore here, so use your own teaching methods to make this an enjoyable activity of being in the moment.

Note for Teachers

Smell is a powerful emotional tool that can be an incredible calming and centering aid for mindfulness. However, for some students who have a history of negative or traumatic experiences, it may be triggering and bring out some sadness or other unexpected and uncomfortable emotions. It is recommended to have your school counselor, social worker, or psychologist sit in on this practice. If that is not possible, keep a keen eye out for visibly upset students, and be familiar with the process of referring them for counseling.

SCENT	NATURAL/PROCESSED	FEELING/EMOTION	MEMORY
Grass	Natural	Fresh air	Playing with friends
Orange peel	Natural	Hungry, stomach growls	Breakfast time
Playdough	Processed	Excited	Art project, after-school fun
Durian fruit (offensive)	Natural	Bad taste in the mouth, squishy stomach	Visiting foreign countries or places
Lavender or lemongrass oil	Processed from flowers	Calm, pleasing	Open air, flowers

ACTIVITY

Using All Your Senses

The purpose of this activity is to have students notice their senses and awareness of what is happening around them. Do this activity before or after a lesson, or during some downtime.

INSTRUCTIONS: Ask students to think about or write down the following:
1. Something they can see
2. Something they can hear
3. Something they can smell
4. Something they can touch
5. Something they can taste

If you are going to have them do this as a mindfulness sitting practice during class, you can ask them to share just one of the senses that they noticed. There are many variations to this activity: For example, instead of having students use all their senses, you can ask them to use one sense, such as seeing. Or they can locate shapes, colors, and objects around the classroom. Browse around the classroom to see what items may be useful for this activity.

Mindful Movement

Some days, just sitting can be challenging, and that is where mindful movement can be a tool for cultivating awareness and focus. Before we learned to run, we had to learn to walk; before we learned to walk, we had to learn how to stand and balance our posture without falling; before we learned to stand and balance, we had to learn to crawl. This is quite a task for a one-year-old. How did we ever learn to walk? Practice, practice, practice. It is the same with mindfulness: to fully understand the benefits, we have to be open and committed to repetitive practice.

Each mindful movement experience is slightly different, but all have the same premise, which is to slow down the chaotic mind and tune in to the body—to be right where you are.

Contributor's Personal Reflection

Throughout my experiences of attending and co-leading mindfulness retreats, there has always been a session for teaching mindful walking. The activity appeals to the mind and body, allowing a sense of adventure or wonderment of where you are now, and where you are going: nowhere!

In Thailand, you often see monks, wearing bright orange robes, walking at daybreak. Part of their spiritual belief of being present is mindful walking. It is amazing to observe their cadence and carefulness of walking barefoot on the roadside or water's edge—the simplicity of taking peaceful strides with slow rhythmic movement, while being unaffected by the chaos around them.

It is stillness in motion, something that you can definitely feel but is difficult to verbalize.

Mindful Walking

PREPARATION: You will need an area large enough for each student to have about 9–10 feet to walk in a straight line. The instructions are to envision an imaginary lane and walk slowly to the end, pause at the end of the lane, slowly turn around, and walk back to the starting point.

INSTRUCTIONS:

1. Tell the children to start with an intention. An intention is similar to a goal, yet it is meant for the present moment, to focus on the immediate task at hand. The intention here is to walk and notice themselves walking.

2. Instruct them to envision an imaginary path or road and walk slowly to the end. Students should drop their gaze downward to their feet and the floor.

3. Then ask them to pause at the end, turn around, and slowly walk back to the starting point.

4. Continue this for about five minutes.

5. You can have students add a mantra or special cues to each phase of movement. For example, they can say "moving" as the lead foot is in motion. Next, they can say "placing" as they gently place the lead foot on the floor, and say "shifting" as the other foot begins to move forward. Moving, placing, shifting, moving, placing, shifting, and so on.

6. You can also have them add breathing to each phase of movement. Tell them, "Lift your foot as you inhale. And exhale as you place your foot down." The purpose is not to *get* anywhere but to focus on the breath and physical sensations in the body as they walk.

7. Remind students that they will most likely notice their mind wandering because this is a repetitive task that can be done automatically. When the autopilot kicks in and the mind wanders, instruct them to bring the intention back to the feet, breath, or movement that is happening in the moment.

It truly is amazing that our bodies know how to walk without even paying attention. Encourage students to try mindful walking on the way to an assembly or lunch. You can also use this activity for launching discussions about gratitude or other autopilot behaviors.

I learned mindful walking while on a 10-day silent meditation retreat. We were encouraged to always walk mindfully anytime we needed to go anywhere. In addition, we took a 30-minute mindful walk every day after lunch. The dedicated nature path passed through a wooded area and circled a lake. I found this to be an easy way to be mindfully present because I was active and it engaged all of my senses in a pleasant, serene, and aesthetic environment.

Nature Walks

There is something about nature that helps us align focus and attention with our direct experience. One current trend is guided "awe walks" that serve as meditation. The sole purpose is to encounter something that makes you feel or say "ah," such as standing amid 2,000-year-old sequoia trees. In Japan, this is called forest bathing or *shinrin-yoku* and is known to restore mood and energy, have physical and psychological benefits, and concretely reduce physiological stress indicators by connecting one's senses with nature (Hansen et al. 2017; Park et al. 2009).

You most likely do not have access to a bamboo forest, but almost any field trip or outdoor activity is not only worth planning but also a good way to refresh and rejuvenate your own meditation practice. What's more, you can bring in other academic subjects—biology, environmental science, ecology, poetry, and self-discovery to name a few.

ACTIVITY

Nature Walk

Nature and the great outdoors often stimulate a sense of wonder, curiosity, and creative imagination, allowing purity of the five senses. Even a single tree or flowering bush around the school can serve as a connection between nature and the human spirit. Notice the texture of a tree's bark, the intricate veins in the leaves of plants, or the smell of flowers. Perhaps observe the pattern of an insect or listen to a bird's song or wings in flight. (Be sure to have your adventure areas inspected for insects and pesticides that may be harmful to the students.)

If you cannot venture outside, consider creating an herb garden in the classroom by planting seeds in pots and placing them on windowsills as a botany-based mindfulness activity. With a little preparation and imagination, your mindful moments can come to life for you and your students.

Critical Thinking!

Do a quick review of the Lesson 2 activities and principles. Discuss with the students how they think their awareness is developing from the activities and discussions they have been introduced to so far. Ask the following questions:

"Have you tried any of the activities at home or with a friend?"

"How do you gather information to stay aware and connected through your senses?"

Add your own questions to gain feedback from your students. If some of the concepts and activities were unclear, consider repeating them before you move on to Lesson 3.

is for Investigate

Explore the physical sensations in the body and what they are trying to tell you

OBJECTIVES

1. Recognize the physical sensations in the body.
2. Develop tools to help students relax when their body is anxious.
3. Explore how the mind and body work together.

THE VOWELS OF MINDFULNESS

See if you can notice what your body feels like right now.

Do you ever feel tense or notice tight muscles when you are annoyed?

Does your heart beat fast or stomach feel squishy before you take a test?

If you notice these sensations, you can investigate them further.

How can you make your body calm and relaxed?

Try the body scan at night to help you calm down or sleep.

I is for Investigate

Are there any physical sensations that you can feel right now?
We call this the "physical sensations" in the body. What does the physical body feel like when you are nervous, excited, tired, happy, or having a strong emotion?

ACTIVITY: Trip around the body/body scan, slow-motion movement, balance—Tree Posture, squeeze and relax.

Introduction

Say that the third vowel is *I*: Investigate. Explain that we listen closely to our bodies to know what is happening inside them.

Investigate and explore. Pay attention to what the body feels like by noticing the physical sensations: hot, cold, tight muscles or tension, fast heartbeat, stomachache, and so on.

The activities in Lesson 3 can help students calm their bodies and notice their anatomy on a deeper level.

LESSON BODY

I is for Investigate

Discussion Question

"Do you know what a *physical sensation* is?"

Ask students some questions about their personal experience of how their body feels at different times of the day.

One of the most identifiable physical sensations is the hunger pang in the stomach they sometimes feel before lunchtime. Describe the different scenarios below and ask students if they notice any physical changes in their bodies as they listen:

- "You are about to take a final exam and are worried you will not pass and will be in trouble for not studying enough." (Example responses: nervous stomach, tight jaw, clenched fists.)

- "You are standing on a cliff looking down. It is very high and even though there is a railing, you feel like you might fall." (Example responses: weak knees, trembling hands, sweaty palms.)

- "It's the last day of school with only 10 minutes until the bell rings, and you get to go to the swimming pool with all your friends after school." (Example responses: rapid heart rate, antsy feet.)

ACTIVITY

Mind and Body Connection

If the budget allows or if your PE teacher has access to them, use heart rate monitoring devices that provide visual biofeedback to demonstrate how *imagining* scenarios can change physical sensations. The more students can understand what is happening in the body, the better prepared they can be to help it remain calm.

Try this group experiment.

PREPARATION: You will need heart rate monitoring devices and a short ghost story—or another kind of thrilling or exciting story.

INSTRUCTIONS:

1. Start by teaching students how to take their pulse or use an instant hand-held pulse device, which you can pass around to each student.

2. Tell the students that you will be dividing them into two groups: one group will stay in the classroom and listen to a ghost story; the other group will walk around outside. Ask them to guess if heart rates will go up, go down, or stay the same.

3. Direct students to take their pulse and record it on the board or in their notebook.

4. Divide the class into two groups:

    Group 1 sits in a circle and listens to a ghost—or thrilling or exciting—story that you have prepared. Perhaps with their eyes closed. (Choose a story that's not *too* scary to avoid triggering unwanted emotions.)

    Group 2 walks around outside for five minutes.

5. Instruct students to reconvene in the classroom, quickly take their pulse again, and record it on the board or in their notebooks.

6. The students' heart rates may or may not match the hypothesis but will certainly stimulate some investigative discussion.

7. Discuss how being still with an active mind can cause the body to react with heightened physical sensations just as with physical exercise. They can write or share their personal experiences.

ACTIVITY

Mind, Body, Go!

"We want children to notice how they're feeling in the moment, not to change the way they feel. When approached in this way, mindfulness often helps children feel calmer and more relaxed but not always." —Susan Kaiser Greenland

Author Susan Kaiser Greenland created a lively and straightforward way for children to notice a connection between what's happening in their minds and bodies in the moment. Mind, Body, Go!* helps with the life skill of focusing.

Children roll a ball back and forth as they quickly name a sensation and an emotion that they are feeling right now. It can be played with or without a ball in partners sitting across from one another, or with a group sitting in a circle (Kaiser Greenland 2016, 107).

*Excerpt reproduced with permission from *Mindful Games* by Susan Kaiser Greenland.

PREPARATION: A small ball and enough floor space for children to sit in a circle

INSTRUCTIONS:

1. "We're going to roll this ball to one another, and when it's your turn, quickly name one thing that you're feeling in your mind and one thing that you're feeling in your body. Here's an example: 'My body feels relaxed, and my mind feels happy.' I'll start: 'My body feels stiff, and my mind feels a little nervous.'"

2. Roll the ball to your partner or to another child in the circle.

3. Tell the person receiving the ball, "Now you name something and roll the ball back." (For example, you could say, "My foot itches, and I feel silly.")

4. Guide the children in speeding up the pace as the play continues.

TEACHER'S TIP: Play Mind, Body, Go! without a ball while sitting around the kitchen table or in the car when you are stuck in traffic.

ACTIVITY

My Mind Feels, My Body Feels

PREPARATION: Stress ball or similar object

Author's Note

I allow the students to pass or hand the stress ball to their neighbor, and we do this fairly quickly. The goal is not as much to share with your classmates but to "check in" with yourself.

INSTRUCTIONS:

1. Ask students to express what physical sensations are present and what is happening in their minds. (Example responses: "My mind feels tired" or busy, confused; "My body feels relaxed" or sore, tingly.)

2. The student then passes the ball to the next person, and so on.

3. This is a good way to check in and become familiar with *thinking* and *sensing* modes.

4. You can do this as "popcorn" (which means anyone can "pop up" an answer) or go around the room in order.

Contributor's Personal Reflection

I love the creativity and effective activities Susan Kaiser Greenland brings to children. I was fortunate to be a mindfulness coach to an 11-year-old girl for eight weeks with one-on-one sessions two times per week. The Mind, Body, Go!

or my version of My Mind Feels, My Body Feels was the icebreaker for us and the best quick activity to get us connected and in the moment. The first time we did the activity, she was reluctant to express herself. I gave her a stress ball to hold while we explored our mind-body feelings. We stuck with it, and by the eighth week, it was a welcoming start to the session. Now, when I see her around town, we always pause and share a quick game of My Mind Feels, My Body Feels with each other. Connections develop with repetition. Remember: be authentic!

Body Scan

PREPARATION: You will need a chime or bell and a timer.

The body scan is a well-known mindfulness practice among adults and can be modified for students. A typical body scan for adults would last about 20–30 minutes, but with children we recommend a condensed version of 5 minutes or less to start—and only if your students can be still for that long.

In the body scan, students are asked a series of short questions that correspond with different parts of the body, beginning with the feet and moving up through the legs, chest, arms, and so on. A trip around the body, so to speak. Throughout the exercise, remind students to notice the breath.

Note for Teachers

This activity is commonly done lying down but can easily be accomplished while students are seated at their desks.

Dim the lights if possible or have natural light for this activity. The premise is to focus on various muscles and body parts while noticing the physical sensations in the body.

You might substitute the word *feelings* in the body if *sensations* is a new word to them. Certainly, feel free to introduce it when you sense your students are ready. Have your chime and timer ready and signal them to begin.

You may feel the need to do the body scan with them and that is fine, granted you have a full view of the class.

Ideally, you have your own mindfulness practices that you engage in at home or whenever and wherever you feel the need to pause. Share personal testimonials of the benefits of your own body scan practice.

One of the key takeaways for students is that they learn to develop this as a tool or technique to calm themselves during periods of anxiety or distress. This practice is quite often useful for preparing the body to sleep.

Micro-scans along with self-check-ins that focus on breathing are excellent for test preparation, performance anxiety, and facing other fears!

During the body scan with students, we suggest you close your eyes periodically, so the students feel you are scanning and practicing body awareness too.

Take glances around the room: if you see students' eyes wandering to others, gently remind them to focus back on their body. It might be helpful to discuss the importance of private time and respect for others as they learn to take a relaxation pause.

Suggested Script

Find a comfortable position in your chair with a mindful posture. [Or, if students are lying on the floor, say, "Find a comfortable position on your back."]

Let your feet and hands rest naturally or what feels comfortable to you. Notice the weight of your body as you are sitting. Let your eyes close or look down if that feels good to you.

Take a few slightly deeper breaths and notice the body being still. During the next few moments, if you have an itch, you can scratch it, but it's best if you can remain very still and relaxed.

First, pay attention to the parts of the body that are contacting the chair [or surface of the floor].

Let's begin with the feet. Pay attention to your feet flat on the floor. Do they feel heavy, hot, cold, tingly? Can you feel your feet in your socks or shoes? Wiggle your toes a little. Can you notice each toe?

[As you move through each body part, allow for a slight pause in silence so they can tune in before continuing.]

We will let the feet rest now and focus our attention on the legs. See if you can notice the left leg calf muscles [pause], *the front of the lower left leg* [pause], *and then the upper leg or thigh muscles. Now, move your attention to the right calf* [pause], *now the front of the lower right leg. And then the upper leg muscles. Do they feel heavy, tired, relaxed? You may not feel anything and that is okay. Just allow yourself to relax and listen to my voice. Let your legs rest now and place one of your hands on your belly and one on your chest. See if you can feel your breath going in and out of your belly. Do you feel your stomach or chest rising as you breathe? Can you feel your heartbeat on your chest? Take a few easy breaths and notice this area of the body.*

Now, let the chest and stomach rest while you move your attention to the head and shoulders. Are your shoulders tight or scrunched up to your ears? See if you can take a breath and let the shoulders relax. Now, let's move to the head. Without touching them, can you notice what the face and head feel like? From the ears, to the eyelids, to the cheekbones, to the nose, and then to the lips and chin. Let your entire head and face relax for a moment.

Now, let go of the head and face and pay attention to your arms. Allow your right arm and left arm from the top of your shoulders to your fingertips to be heavy and relaxed.

Take a breath and simply notice what your body feels like now. Take one more scan around the body, stopping at any area you want, and just continue to notice any sensations and your breathing.

[Pause]

Allow the whole body to relax for a moment. Soon we will be finished with this body scan, and I will sound the chime. Start to wiggle your toes and fingers and let a smile be on your face.

[Ring the chime]

Students will most likely begin to stretch their bodies and sigh a few breaths as you slowly add more light back to the room. You can opt to discuss this practice or simply move on to the next segment of your class. After being still for a while, they may need some form of mobility, art expression, or group learning.

ACTIVITIES

Mindful Body Balance

Our human bodies are built for movement, and sitting at a table or desk for hours a day is not beneficial for the body. Here are six quick body awareness "wake ups" for students to try standing next to their desks.

Contributor's Note

I have found that teaching balance movements is a positive way to help students regain focus, release stress hormones, and get the creative juices flowing.

INSTRUCTIONS: For each balance activity below, read the directions and demonstrate the movements.

Still Mountain

1. Stand up straight and still like a mountain. Place your feet slightly wider than hip-width apart. Keep your arms and hands at your sides.
2. Envision in your mind that your feet are the base of a strong and stable mountain.
3. Take a few slow easy breaths.
4. See if you can feel your feet on the floor. This is your mountain base that keeps you firmly planted on the earth's floor.
5. Imagine the wind is blowing across your face, but you do not move because you are a strong, still mountain.
6. Continue to breathe and focus on being tall, still, and strong.
7. Repeat the following mantra out loud or to yourself: "I am strong and still like a mountain."

Flamingo

1. Stand up tall like a flamingo bird with feet hip-width apart.
2. Lift the right leg six inches off the ground in front of you and stand as still as you can for 10 seconds.
3. Return with both feet on the floor and take a few breaths.
4. Slowly lift the right leg up again and move it to the side and hold for 10 seconds.
5. Next gradually move the right leg behind you and hold for 10 seconds.
6. If you lose your balance, simply place your foot on the ground and slowly lift again.
7. Repeat the sequence with the left leg.

Obviously, this is an exercise in physical balance, yet the mind is the most important aspect of it. Encourage students to try not to judge themselves if they slip and to just keep coming back to the pose. We often lose our balance when our minds begin to wander or get distracted. Tell them that when they notice their focus has moved away, simply follow their breath and bring it back.

Sumo Wrestler

1. Stand with your feet wide apart and point your feet slightly outward.
2. Place your hands on your knees.
3. Bend your knees.
4. Lean to one side and lift your leg, stomp it down, and do the same with the other leg.

Downhill Skier

1. Stand tall with your feet close together.
2. Bend at your knees.
3. Rest your forearms on your thighs and make loose fists with both hands.
4. Keep a straight spine, look forward, and envision yourself skiing down a mountain.

Rag Doll

It is important to do counterbalance postures for good body balance. After doing an upright posture, do a 20-second rag doll in between. (Envision Sheriff Woody from the movie *Toy Story*.)

1. Stand up tall with feet hip-width apart.
2. Slowly bend forward from the hips.

3. Allow your upper body to lean down with your fingertips toward the floor (don't push or bounce).

4. Hang down relaxed like a rag doll.

If your class is advanced or familiar with other stretching or balancing techniques, you can add them anytime.

Use a "Simon says" approach (a student picks a pose and leads the class) to make it more playful or to encourage some leadership.

Tall Tree

1. Stand up tall like a tree with feet hip-width apart.
2. Envision in your mind that your feet are the base of a tree with roots firmly planted into the earth.
3. Take a few slow easy breaths.
4. Place one foot on your ankle, or on the inside of your thigh.
5. Slowly bring your arms up straight overhead with palms touching.
6. Hold for a few seconds.

Special Contributor's Note

This activity is often called the Tree Pose, a yoga position that some school administrations may object to. Make it clear that you are not teaching a yoga class; emphasize that this is a mind and body balancing activity.

Challenge

Encourage students to try the balance postures at home and invite their family or friends to give it a try.

Stress and the Body

We may perceive stress as being only in our minds. However, it manifests itself in the body as well and can have devastating health consequences (Yaribeygi et al. 2017). Have you ever noticed someone massaging their shoulders or neck while talking about how stressed they are? There is something called the "stress triangle" where the muscles in the neck, shoulders, and face tighten up when stress is happening in the mind (UWSHS 2018). Many do not even notice how it is affecting the body. Noticing the physical body by intentionally bringing awareness to it is important when feeling stressed. If constant stress or repeated stressors happen in the mind, chances are the body is in turmoil and in need of some relief as well.

BRAIN SCIENCE

Your memory is a record of the past, although it is not always an accurate recorder. When you remember something, it is very similar to actually experiencing the past, and it will most likely be accompanied by emotions. Similarly, when you think about the future, your brain can imagine what might happen. This too is likely to trigger emotions.

When you come into the "here and now," which is what all these mindfulness exercises are designed to do, you set aside thoughts of the people, things, or places that may be causing your problems. When you are truly present (not judging in any way), you will be surprised at how little is actually going on, moment to moment. This opens the mind for clarity and focus.

There is a misconception that stress is caused by outside circumstances. In fact, stress is caused by your individual degree of reactivity. In other words, stress is caused by what you think and how you feel about different situations. You store memories in the part of your brain that is very close to the area responsible for survival (our fight, flight, and freeze response). We will explore this in more detail next.

Amygdala, Hippocampus, Prefrontal Cortex

There are three regions of the brain that influence physical sensations, emotions, and reactions: the amygdala, hippocampus, and prefrontal cortex. Understanding their functions and how they interact will help you to understand the stress response and how mindfulness can be beneficial.

Scientists report that these regions of the brain can change and improve by being mindful (Bauer et al. 2019; Hölzel et al. 2011; Thierry et al. 2016), more specifically through meditation and stillness. While the evidence of this is more limited in children than adults, more recent studies (e.g., Bauer) are showing promising results in children. In fact, there has already been a growing body of literature showing its effectiveness and that it can improve both executive function and cognitive skills in children (Weare 2012). We feel confident that if teachers plant the seeds of mindfulness and give students the tools to control their attention and emotional regulation, they will benefit later in life.

Essentially, the three regions mentioned above can be explained as follows:

The amygdala: This portion of the brain is known as the fight or flight center. It is the primary region associated with fear and emotions (Davis and Whalen 2000; Ressler 2010). With mindfulness, it is said to shrink or become smaller (Hölzel et al. 2009), causing less reactivity to fear. This is not to say we are emotionless or will not react to danger, but we will be able to have a clearer picture of what is real and what needs attending to. For example, if you are walking in the woods and see something that looks like a snake, the immediate reaction would be fear; you will either freeze or run away. When you are mindful, you can have a deeper look.

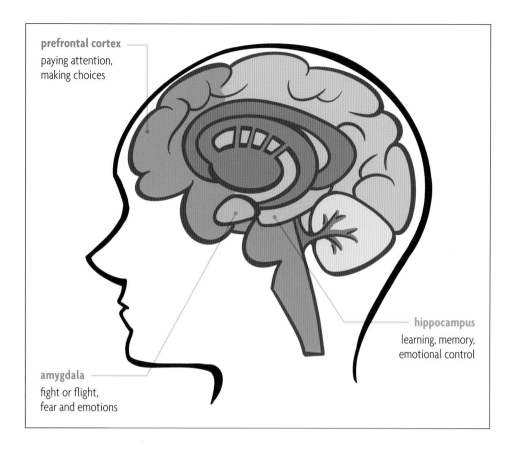

prefrontal cortex
paying attention, making choices

hippocampus
learning, memory, emotional control

amygdala
fight or flight, fear and emotions

Hippocampus: This part of the brain grows larger with mindfulness (Hölzel et al. 2011) and is "critically involved in learning and memory processes, and in the modulation of emotional control" (37). The hippocampus is directly involved in executive function (Blair 2017).

Prefrontal cortex: This part helps with making choices and paying attention so we can grasp knowledge (Fuster 2008).

The Blissful Kids website has a Mindfulness and the Brain Made Easy page that offers posters and excellent illustrations for younger students to learn about this topic.

Multitasking

Since we are focusing on *I* for Investigation, let's look a little closer at our cognitive brain, the one that gets tasks done.

You've heard the term *multitasking*—but is there such a thing? It turns out there is no such thing as multitasking in the physical sense, and it does not work (Kubu and Machado 2017). Rather, people are more prone to making mistakes and become less efficient when they attempt to multitask (APA 2006). The word *multitasking* is common in the workplace, but it is slowly being replaced with more accurate terms such as *uni-tasking* or *attention shifting*.

We like to introduce this to older students especially because they firmly believe they can do multiple things at once. And in a way, they can. It is just not as effective as paying attention to one thing at a time (APA 2006). We do know that shifting from one thing to another can lead to more mistakes (APA) and might cause fatigue. Mindfulness, on the other hand, can enhance our ability to stay focused on one task at a time. Now, let's practice more fun mindfulness activities.

Squeeze and Relax*

The squeeze and relax exercises are designed to relieve muscle tension and tune in to the body. They are based on Progressive Muscle Relaxation (PMR), which has solid scientific evidence in reducing anxiety, panic, phobias, and stress, in addition to increasing physical and mental well-being (Mackereth and Tomlinson 2010). We use a version borrowed from Koeppen (1974).

The exercise asks students to tense a body part and then relax it on your command. They tighten the body part for 5 seconds and then relax for 10 seconds. Repeat. This exercise will help your students learn to identify tight muscles and how to relax when they are feeling anxious or stressed. Tensing and relaxing different muscles in the body can help your students learn the difference between being tense and feeling relaxed (Koeppen).

Note for Teachers

Be sure to tell students to squeeze hard enough to make the muscle tight but not painful.

Lemon Squeeze (ARMS AND HANDS)

Extend both arms straight out in front of you. Pretend you are squeezing a whole lemon in each hand. Squeeze the lemons as best you can without straining. Feel the tightness in your hands and arms as you squeeze. Now drop the lemon and relax. See how much better your hands and arms feel when they are relaxed.

Turtle (SHOULDERS)

Pretend you are a turtle. You're sitting out on a rock by a nice, peaceful pond, just relaxing in the warm sun. It feels nice and warm and safe here. Oh-oh! You sense danger. Pull your head into your house [pull your shoulders up to your ears]. Hold for five

*Reproduced with permission (Koeppen 1974, 14–21).

seconds. The danger has passed now. You can come out and once again relax and feel the warm sunshine.

Elephant Steps on Your Stomach (ABDOMINALS)

Hey! Here comes a cute baby elephant. But he's not watching where he's going. He doesn't see you lying there in the grass, and he's about to step on your stomach. Don't move. You don't have time to get out of the way. Just get ready for him. Make your stomach very hard. Tighten up your stomach muscles real tight. Hold it. It looks like he is going the other way. You can relax now. Let your stomach go soft. Let it be as relaxed as you can.

Fly on Your Nose (FACE AND NOSE)

Here comes a pesky old fly. He has landed on your nose. Try to get him off without using your hands. That's right, wrinkle up your nose. Make as many wrinkles in your nose as you can. Scrunch your nose up real hard. Good. You've chased him away. Now you can relax your nose.

Feet in the Mud (LEGS AND FEET)

Now pretend that you are standing barefoot in a big, fat mud puddle. Squish your toes down deep into the mud. Try to get your feet down to the bottom of the mud puddle. Push down, spread your toes apart, and feel the mud squish up between your toes. Scrunch your feet in the mud like your mom doesn't care. Now step out of the mud puddle. Relax your feet. Let your toes go loose, and feel how nice that is. It feels good to be relaxed.

Squeeze through the Fence (WHOLE BODY)

Stand tall and rigid like a mummy. Tighten your whole body at once. You are playing with your friends next door, and you hear the dinner bell signaling you to come home. The gate is locked so you can't get out. You see a small crack in the fence, so you squeeze through just in time for dinner. Whew! Exhale and relax all your muscles.

Critical Thinking!

- Do a quick review of the Lesson 3 activities and learning principles.

- Ask the students about how they feel in this moment. What does the physical body feel like when they are nervous, excited, tired, or happy?

- Discuss how they can connect what happens in their body (how they feel) to what happens in their minds (what they think).

Challenge

Encourage students to try the body scan at night to help calm down or sleep.

is for Observe

Notice your thoughts, feelings, and emotions and how to respond to them

OBJECTIVES

1. Learn to observe your thoughts and explore how your mind wanders.
2. Learn how you can use mindfulness to control anger and refrain from doing something that you might regret.
3. Learn the difference between reacting and responding.
4. Recognize the difference between a thought and a fact.
5. Learn how to create a space between a strong emotion and an action.
6. Develop tools to choose your best action.

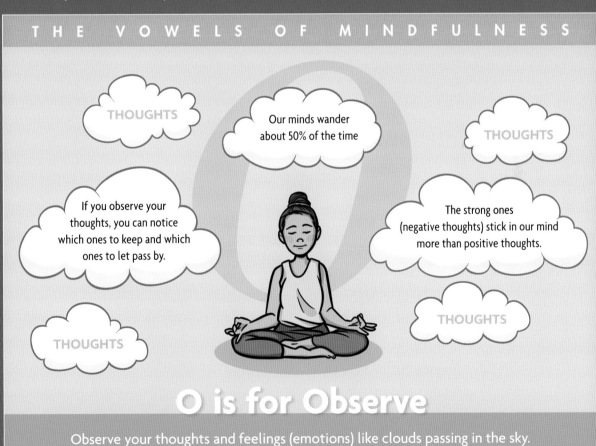

THE VOWELS OF MINDFULNESS

THOUGHTS

Our minds wander about 50% of the time

THOUGHTS

If you observe your thoughts, you can notice which ones to keep and which ones to let pass by.

The strong ones (negative thoughts) stick in our mind more than positive thoughts.

THOUGHTS

THOUGHTS

O is for Observe

Observe your thoughts and feelings (emotions) like clouds passing in the sky.

"Between stimulus and response is a space. In that space you have the power to choose your response."

VIKTOR FRANKL

THOUGHTS

Let's say this is anger. Hold up one finger.

And this is our reaction. Hold up one finger from the opposite hand right next to the anger finger.

Without mindfulness, these two fingers (my anger and my action) are right next to each other.

Where there is mindfulness, it comes between these two fingers and pushes them apart so that the action is not close to the anger.

Mindfulness helps create a space between a strong emotion and our action. Mindfulness creates that space so we can make a different decision.

Introduction

Say that the fourth vowel is *O*: Observe.

O is for Observe

Thoughts, Thoughts, Thoughts: The Good, the Bad, and the Ugly

Every day, we have thousands of thoughts. Many of them are the same thought over and over. Of those repetitive thoughts, the majority are often negative. The strong, negative thoughts tend to stick in our minds more than the positive thoughts.

Psychologist Rick Hanson states that "the brain is like Velcro for negative experiences, but Teflon for positive ones" (Hanson 2018). Velcro is sticky, and Teflon—like in a frying pan—is slick. The good thoughts slide by (Teflon), and the negative ones stick in our heads (Velcro). There is actually an evolutionary reason for this: negative events (such as an attack by a wildcat) need to be paid much more attention to than positive events in order to help us survive. However, in the modern world, most of the time kids are not facing life-threatening events.

Most people do not realize that the mind can actually tell us some wonderful stories; it is a storytelling machine. Unfortunately, the story is often not a great one, often full of negativity and judgments. Why does this happen? It is simple—it all has to do with our brain's survival instinct.

In the past, the amygdala and survival parts of the brain (remember Lesson 3) were busy helping us survive by protecting us from predators and finding food and shelter. Real threats. These days, most of us are so lucky to live great lives where we have all our basic needs met and much more. What that means is our minds get busy worrying about other stuff.

For example, if someone was mean to you once, and it caused a reaction in your mind or body, the chances are that same thought and emotion will repeat for you for a long time and possibly throughout your life. The mind thinks there is a threat. However, this time the threat is more emotional and psychological rather than based on life or death. The brain sets in motion to release all the necessary chemicals you may need to fight, flight, or freeze (APA 2018; McCorry 2007).

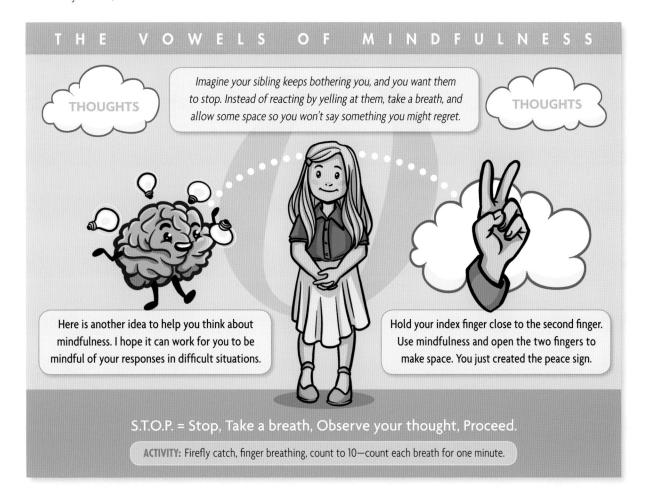

You can see this in your daily life: people arguing, experiencing road rage, crawling into bed for days at a time, or freezing before public speaking. When we are in *fight, flight, or freeze* mode, our sympathetic nervous system is highly activated (McCorry 2007). If we live in this system for too long, our well-being and health can be compromised (APA 2018).

Such a powerful understanding of our brain shows us that we are being pulled and pushed around by the amygdala. Therefore, we are not always rational in our thinking. With mindfulness to help us relax and be calm, we are able to activate the parasympathetic nervous system (Alpart 2019) and create some space between our immediate and our instinctive reactions, thereby allowing us to observe our thoughts, feeling, and emotions. We then have the power to pause and reflect before we act.

Negative thoughts are very common and normal, even among young children. Negative thinking can trigger many uncomfortable emotions for them. Allowing negative thoughts to hang out all the time in your head might lead to feeling unhappy, angry, moody, or worse.

Imagine three kids—Josefina, Waya, and Malee—have a plan to go play in the park tomorrow. When they wake up the next day, they see that it is snowing. Josefina thinks, "Oh no! This ruins everything. I can't go to the park and have fun." She feels sad, disappointed, and angry. Waya thinks, "Oh, wonderful. I can play in the snow at the park." He feels happy, excited, and hopeful. Malee, on the other hand, just thinks, "Oh, snow." She has no emotional reaction.

The same situation can be viewed differently depending on how you think about it, and you have the power to choose what you think. Which means you also have a choice about how you feel. Negative thoughts take you away from the present, which does not allow you to enjoy the here and now.

Mindfulness can be used to observe your thoughts without judging them and focus your attention on the present moment. If you try to simply observe your thoughts before reacting to them, you can notice which ones to keep and which ones to let go of.

Think of your thoughts like a leaf traveling down a stream or clouds passing in the sky.

TEACHER'S TIP: For younger ones, blowing soap bubbles may be a good way to illustrate thoughts moving around.

Note for Teachers

Thoughts can have a superpower of their own. They can hijack your mind and cloud reality. This can cause emotional turmoil.

Have you ever been involved in a stressful incident and required to write a report and state only the facts? Or perhaps there was a conflict between a coworker, a parent, or someone where a mediator was needed to help resolve the situation. It is so hard to just state the facts, especially if the incident is fresh on the mind with emotions flaring.

So, while these practices of listing thoughts versus facts are important and necessary, they can be hard to grasp and even harder to put into practice. Be patient and allow some space.

ACTIVITY

Thoughts versus Facts

The purpose of this activity is to use scenarios to illustrate how our thoughts impact the storyline in our minds.

INSTRUCTIONS: Read the story aloud—or prerecord an audio—so the students can sit and listen, and/or let them work in groups to solve the mystery.

TEACHER'S TIP: This scenario uses the name Johnny. Please substitute a name that is ethnically appropriate for your school or audience.

The Case of the Stolen Backpack

As Johnny walked to school, he was thinking rapidly and feeling stressed about a project he had to present in front of his class that day. He had prepared long and hard yet still didn't feel ready. As he was walking, he remembered that he had forgotten to return the milk to the fridge, which wasn't like him. And to top it off, he noticed his socks were two different colors.

When Johnny got to school, he went straight to the teacher's desk, set down his backpack, pulled out his homework, and placed the homework on the teacher's desk. He then went to the back of the room and hung his coat on the hook, as he always did.

Next, Johnny sat at his desk and took a few deep breaths. But still, his mind was on the terrible things that had happened this morning. The teacher from the class next door came in and looked directly at Johnny as she was talking with his teacher. He just "knew" it was about him and that he was in trouble.

At recess time, he went to the back of the class to get his coat, and his backpack was gone.

"This has got to be the worst day ever," Johnny thought.

Can you be a detective and determine the facts?

1. Was Johnny's backpack missing?

   ANSWER: *Yes, it was missing from his mind as to where he placed it.*

2. Did someone steal his backpack?

   ANSWER: *No; however, his recall was hijacked by his nervous system.*

3. What happened to his backpack? Just the facts, please.

   ANSWER: *He left it by the teacher's desk.*

The answers are obvious when you read them, but so often our thoughts get hijacked, so we do not see the facts.

As a teacher, you can modify the story and add your own reflective questions.

Below are other scenarios you may want to use to facilitate a discussion about the thoughts-versus-facts phenomenon. Students can share their experiences and brainstorm reliable solutions.

1. My friend did not reply to my text message.
2. My teammate never tosses the ball to me during basketball practice.
3. A friend walked right past me in the hall and turned her head the other way.

Thoughts Are Not Facts

"It is remarkable how liberating it feels to be able to see that your thoughts are just thoughts and that they are not 'you' or 'reality.'" –Jon Kabat-Zinn (2013).

ACTIVITY

The Tale of Two Wolves

The Tale of Two Wolves (Yeo 2016) is a popular legend of unknown origin that illustrates our good and bad thoughts. This tale is a good teaching lesson on how we choose to respond to our thoughts.

PREPARATION: Check out the tale from your school library or retrieve it from the internet to ensure you have a version suitable for your students.

INSTRUCTIONS:

1. Read the story aloud (or prerecord an audio) so students can sit and listen, and then allow them to work in small groups to discuss the meaning.

2. Use art as a form of expression or other skillful techniques for understanding our thoughts and how to respond to them.

3. Discuss the meaning of the tale with your students and help them explore how they can choose which thoughts to pay more attention to and which ones to dismiss.

Viktor Frankl, a Holocaust Survivor

Viktor Frankl was a psychiatrist and holocaust survivor who lived in concentration camps for three years. He endured difficult physical and emotional states while imprisoned, yet his attitude was remarkable, given his circumstances. Being physically strong was not nearly as important as being mentally strong.

In his book *Man's Search for Meaning* (1946), Frankl described how he was able to look within himself, to think of things that brought him joy, and to be grateful for the small things like a bit of mercy from the prison guards or finding peace in a sunset. Instead of getting swept away by negative thoughts, he chose to focus on the positive ones and sought ways to show compassion to others. As a starving man, he found joy in giving his life-sustaining food to others.

Have you ever heard the phrase "mind over matter"? Viktor Frankl was efficient in not letting negative or unwanted thoughts take over his mind, having realized it would cause more distress. He said, in part, "Between stimulus and response is a space. In the space, you have the power to choose."

The meaning is profound. Essentially, he is saying we can decide how we want to respond, and a positive response is usually a more favorable one.

Further research on Frankl's life and his full quote may be applicable and a good history lesson.

You can follow the directions below to demonstrate how mindfulness creates space between reactions and actions.

Let's take the emotion "anger." Hold up one finger and say, "This is our anger." Hold up a finger from the opposite hand right next to the anger finger and say, "This is my action."

Without mindfulness, these two fingers (my anger and my action) are right next to each other. Where there is mindfulness, it comes between these two fingers and pushes them apart so that the action is not close to the anger. Mindfulness creates space so we can make a different decision.

Here is another way to demonstrate allowing space between reacting and action. Hold up your hand with your palm facing the class.

Hold your index finger close to the middle finger on one hand while dropping the other fingers to your palm. Then use mindfulness to make space between the two fingers.

You just created the peace sign.

Say, "Mindfulness is my superpower!"

How's the Weather in Your Mind?

Y ou can view whatever is going on in the mind like the weather. One moment it is stormy, then a brilliant sun appears. Overcast might be a cloudy day or just a dull mind. It comes and goes and, if we watch it, we may notice that it can change. We do not have to stay stuck on one cloud; we can simply watch the clouds go by.

Sometimes our thoughts carry us away and tell a story that is not completely accurate. One of my favorite phrases that helps keep me flowing and not getting stuck on a negative thought is "You don't have to believe everything you think."

You can also observe the body as with the *I* vowel (Investigate). Is there tension or tightness in your face, shoulders, or stomach? Maybe a quick body scan is in order.

STOP

It can be helpful to pause sometimes and pay attention to "what is going on around you and inside your body" (Bonfil 2014). It is a good time to check on your thoughts and feelings too.

It often helps to visualize in your mind the actual image of a STOP sign. The meaning of the red-and-white octagon is known throughout the world.

Dr. Elisha Goldstein says:

> STOP is an acronym that I've adapted from the Mindfulness-Based Stress Reduction (MBSR) program and one of the most popular methods for helping the mind remember how to drop into and expand a space of awareness. The name of this one-minute practice stands for:
>
> **S**top • **T**ake a breath • **O**bserve your body, emotions, and thoughts • **P**roceed to what is most important (2012, 211)

STOP, a road-tested mindfulness practice, can be introduced to older students and done several times a day. It only takes a minute.

INSTRUCTIONS:

1. Explain that we use a technique called STOP to pause and observe what's happening around and within us.

2. Review the acronym: Stop. Take a breath. Observe your body, emotions, and thoughts. Proceed to what's important.

3. Give students a quick example: "Imagine your sibling keeps bothering you and you want them to quit. Instead of reacting by yelling, take a breath and allow some space so you won't say something you regret."

4. Now try it with the students: "We are going to take a STOP break. Sit upright with your mindful posture. Stop and close your eyes if you feel comfortable with them closed. Take a breath, slow and easy. Then take another, and breathe a little deeper this time. Observe what you are thinking right now. Observe how your body feels. That's it! We are done, and now proceed on with your day."

Contributor's Personal Reflection

Sometimes a STOP gives us more appreciation and helps us to be present. I like to purposely STOP when something tantalizes my senses. It might be something pleasing to my eyes like a butterfly or bird in flight, my favorite color on someone's clothes, an interesting aroma, or a melodious song.

The other day I was sitting outside and noticed a stunning blue-colored bird in flight. I paused, took a few breaths, and noticed my feelings.

It was a bluebird and it made me happy. Hence the bluebird of happiness.

The following activities can help students recognize their emotions and observe the habits of their thought patterns and expressions.

Body Language

Before teaching the Feelings Charades activity, you may want to have a conversation with the class about body language.

Keep in mind that with trauma-sensitive students, the actions and expressions may be totally different.

1. State that we are all different and express ourselves in a variety of ways. Sometimes we hide our emotions too.

2. Pick an emotion (e.g., excited) and ask the class to demonstrate, using their own body language, what excitement looks like.

3. State that emotions can be tricky to understand, and sometimes a person's body language gives you clues about how they are feeling.

4. Ask them if they can recall a time when they noticed someone's negative body language without them speaking.

5. How did they respond? Suggest that sometimes we may give unfavorable responses that lead to regret, like "You had a frown on your face, so I frowned back."

6. Lead a discussion about seeking better ways to respond in the future.

7. Ask, "If you don't understand someone's body language, how can you understand their feelings?"

8. Give some examples of how you can find out if someone feels sad or frustrated and what you can do to help.

ACTIVITY

Feelings Charades

The purpose of this activity is to help students identify different emotions and recognize those feelings in their classmates. Ultimately, they want to use the information to be a supportive and understanding peer who is a good listener.

PREPARATION: Gather five index cards and write a different one-word emotion on each card. If possible, choose a word from your current vocabulary lesson.

1. Ask for five volunteers to play as actors of different emotions.

2. Let the five actors draw a card. (Allow flexibility: If an actor has a specific emotion or feeling they really want to share, that is also okay. You know your students and what works best for your classroom dynamics.)

3. Allow them to step outside the classroom or in a corner area to practice their nonverbal expression of their assigned emotion.

4. Each actor will take turns acting out the emotion word while the class takes turns guessing the emotion.

5. When the correct emotion is guessed, write the emotion on the board for all to see.

DISCUSSION POINTS OR ACTIVITIES:

- For people of all ages, understanding how another person may be feeling in a given situation increases the likelihood of a more favorable response, such as care and kindheartedness.

- Talk with the class about the importance of recognizing other people's feelings and how they can respond to them.

- Give some examples of how you can find out if someone seems sad or frustrated and what you can do to help.

- Lead a discussion about seeking better ways to respond in the future.

- Create your own emotion chart or have students draw their own and display them in your classroom.

DISCUSSION QUESTIONS:

- "What were the clues that helped you figure out what the other person is feeling?"

- "What did you notice about their body language or facial expressions?"

- "If you don't understand someone's body language, how can you determine their feelings?"

- "Can you recall a time when you noticed someone's body language without them speaking? How did you respond?"

ACTIVITY

Do You See What I See? Fun with Images

Oftentimes images can be interpreted in different ways, just as body language and facial expressions can be interpreted differently. To help students open up about their own expressions, consider sharing pictures of ambiguous images such as the rabbit and the duck provided by the Art of Play website (artofplay.com/blogs/articles/fun-with-ambiguous-images), or similar optical illusions. These help students realize that we all can see things in a variety of ways and have varying perspectives. This could lead to a discussion about how we perceive things. Students really engage in viewing illusions and ambiguous images.

Before you begin, remind them to be kind and respectful of others' perceptions. Perhaps first do a brief compliment circle (share one thing you like about someone) or have students smile at each other to get them in a positive and complimentary mode.

A C T I V I T Y

Choosing Your Path

The poem "Autobiography in Five Short Chapters" by Portia Nelson (1993) is an analogy representing the choices we make in life. When we make choices, we create our own path. It is about self-awareness. It illustrates our patterns and behaviors and how it takes time to learn how to modify them to make a new decision.

1. Check out the poem from your school library or find it online.
2. It can be printed and read silently with reflection worksheets that can lead to a discussion.
3. You can read it to the class a few times, then discuss the meaning.
4. Invite five volunteers to stand among their peers and read each act of the poem, and then have a group discussion.

DISCUSSION POINTS: After the poem has been read, explain what scientists call the *negativity bias* in our brains (Moore 2019). This bias is meant to protect us from lions and tigers. It is an evolutionary inheritance from our ancestors, a way of protecting us from danger.

Have you ever seen a stick on the sidewalk and thought it was a snake?

That is our brain honoring its role to keep us safe. It is in our genetic make-up. We are predisposed to these genes; therefore, seeing the positive takes more effort. Our brains tend to prioritize negative experiences, oftentimes resulting in uncomfortable emotions that are geared at protecting us.

We are in control, and we control the choices we make one at a time. If you continue to make the same choices, you will get the same results.

If you consciously decide to make new and possibly better choices, your path will begin to change.

Allow students to share their experiences through dialogue or in small groups.

Finger Breathing

This method, which helps students focus and calm themselves, works for all age groups.

INSTRUCTIONS:

1. First, hold your nondominant hand up in the air in front of you, with your palm side facing away from your body.

2. Now take your dominant hand (usually the one you write with) and trace the outline of your fingers.

3. Take your index finger, sometimes called the pointer finger, and begin tracing at the base of your wrist on the opposite hand up toward your thumb.

4. As your index finger runs along the outside of your thumb, breathe in. As it drops down the other side of your thumb, breathe out.

5. As your index finger runs along the outside of your pointer finger, breathe in. As it drops down the other side of your pointer finger, breathe out.

6. Keep up this pattern of tracing all your fingers while matching your breaths to the movements.

You can start with simple tracing if combining breathing with tracing of the fingers feels like too much at once. Even the simple act of tracing can help students to focus and calm down. There are plenty of videos on the internet with explanations if you need more visuals.

TEACHER'S TIP: Students may try to do this very fast. Remind them that the *tracing* follows the *breathing*.

Contributor's Personal Reflection

A few hours after I taught the Finger Breathing practice, I asked the students to sit in their mindful posture, follow their breath, and be as still as they could for one minute. I noticed one student with his hands in his lap slowly tracing his fingers as he followed the in and out of his breath.

My heart filled with joy as I observed his attention and willingness to welcome these new techniques of being attentive. He totally got it.

All hail to mindfulness!

Count to 10

We can all count to 10, but there is a tricky part to this activity. It requires a sense of curiosity with a willingness to explore the busyness of the mind and self-compassion when training your brain. Your students will improve with practice as they grow more mindful. You, too, can practice this activity with them. Make it more playful than competitive!

INSTRUCTIONS:

1. Close your eyes with your mindful posture and begin to count to 10 by following your breath.
2. Breathe in and silently say, "1"; breathe out and say, "1." Breathe in ("2") and breathe out ("2"), breathe in ("3") and breathe out ("3"), and so on.
3. Be sure to breathe with your natural breathing rhythm. Do this for about one minute or until you can get to 10.
4. *The tricky part*: Each time your mind starts to think of something else ("I wonder what is for lunch today." "I miss my cat." "Is that a bird?"), you gently come back and start with the last number you remember.
5. Try not to get carried away by an emotion (frustration, anxiety, sadness). Just keep practicing for one minute.

Isn't it amazing how much our minds wander?

Firefly Catch

We refer to a wandering mind as the monkey mind, puppy mind, busy bee, or what is sometimes called the "firefly mind."

What do all these have in common? Anything that moves about is difficult to catch, right?

Fireflies are beetles that are sometimes called lightning bugs. They light up when they are looking for a mate or to protect themselves from predators (*National Geographic* 2018). We can use the image of catching fireflies like catching ourselves in thought.

INSTRUCTIONS:

1. In the Firefly Catch activity, you sit with your mindful posture and begin to pay attention to your breathing.

2. Every time your mind wanders off to thinking, you raise your cupped hand in the air to catch the thought.

3. Slowly bring your hand back to your body or just open it and let the thought go, and then return to following your breathing.

TEACHER'S TIP: Do the practice with them and note the abundance of fireflies you catch!

Challenge

Encourage students to practice these activities with a friend or family member: Firefly Catch, Finger Breathing, Count to 10.

Critical Thinking!

- Do a quick review of the Lesson 4 activities and learning principles.
- Explore with students what it is like to observe their thoughts.
- Ask them to discuss situations where they can use mindfulness to prevent themselves from saying or doing something they might regret based on their emotional reaction.

is for Understand

Learn how to be kind to yourself and others with compassion and gratitude

OBJECTIVES

1. Learn what it feels like to be grateful.
2. Imagine what you can do to show some gratitude.

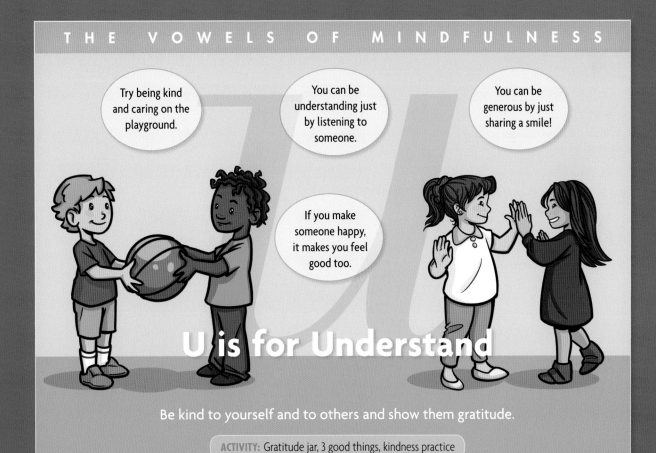

Introduction

There are a lot of ways to be understanding. When you begin to explore this vowel, you may find that the list can be endless.

You can be understanding by:

1. Listening to someone with your full attention
2. Purposely being kind and caring in the lunchroom or on the playground
3. Offering to share a favorite color crayon or pencil
4. Being generous by just sharing a smile!
5. Showing gratitude with positive responses like "please" and "thank you"

If you make someone happy, it will make you feel good too.

REMEMBER: It is important to be kind to yourself as well.

LESSON BODY
U is for Understand

Say that the fifth vowel is *U*: Understand.

Explain that we will now discover how kindness helps everybody, and how to be grateful and show gratitude.

Key words: *kindness, gratitude, grateful, compassion, thankfulness.*

Before you engage in the activities, you may want to introduce your students to the topic of *understanding*.

Suggested Script

Has this ever happened to you? You do something kind for someone without even thinking about it. Maybe you open a door for someone or ask someone if they need help. Or you pick up something that someone has dropped.

After the act is over, you feel a surge of energy; perhaps a smile appears on your face. Can you think of other things you have done to be kind to someone?

This is called random acts of kindness and it is a science! Yes, I said "science" and will explain more later.

Below are several activities to create small moments of gratitude every day.

Farm to Fork (aka "Grapeful")

Begin by telling the story of how a seed becomes food. In this story, draw attention to all the aspects that students can be grateful for, including the people who plant the seeds, the sunlight and water needed to make the seeds grow, the people or machines that harvest it, and the resources needed to transport it. By having a better understanding of the elements involved in food production, children may realize all the people and processes that they can be grateful for.

PREPARATION: Wash a bunch of grapes, and make sure everyone's hands are sanitized before touching the grapes. (Important: make sure no one has a grape allergy.)

INSTRUCTIONS:

1. Pass around one grape to each student. Use something like muffin cups or paper towels to keep the surfaces clean and grapes from rolling around.
2. Allow students to observe the grape but not eat it yet.
3. Next, ask students to describe how they think the grape got from the vineyard to their classroom. What people and things were required? (Example responses: sunlight, water, harvesting, people to transport.)
4. Tell students to begin their answers with "I am grateful for . . ."
5. Encourage them to be thankful every day for at least one thing that helped bring food to their lunch box, school cafeteria, or dinner table.

This activity is especially appropriate in late fall when many are celebrating Thanksgiving.

Contributor's Note

The first time I led the Farm to Fork activity, I placed a grape on each student's desk and told them this was a lesson on gratitude. I was a little nervous when thinking about how I could convince them to be grateful for one silly grape. One student blurted out, "I get it. We need to be 'grapeful.'" To this day I am not sure if he misspoke or if it was a profound epiphany. We all had a laugh and attention participation soared.

ACTIVITY

Kind Thoughts Practices

Note for Teachers

Kind thoughts are sometimes called loving-kindness, and the word *loving-kindness* is rooted in the Buddhist tradition of friendliness. Although this guidebook's lesson plans and activities are secular, many concepts have ancient roots. The purpose of this activity is to send good thoughts to someone and has no religious meanings or undertones. It is simply a way to offer well wishes. Keep in mind that this activity can bring on strong emotions, especially for trauma-sensitive students. Having the school counselor, psychologist, or social worker present provides a safety net for the students. Use positive words during the instructions of the practice: *please*, *kindly*, and *thank you*. Also, use a calm and quiet voice, and carefully choose simple words for the children to recite: *happy*, *healthy*, *safe*, *peaceful*, *at ease*. We use *protected* because some students may live in dangerous neighborhoods and may not feel safe, but if they have loving people around them, they can feel protected.

Suggested Script: Kind Thoughts 1

This kindness practice requires the use of your imagination. I will be asking you to please think of someone positive. It might be someone you see often and who makes you happy every time you see them. It is important that this person is someone you see almost every day so you can have a clear picture in your mind. If you do not have a person right now, you can think of a pet, plant, or tree.

In this activity, I will invite you to send kind thoughts to the one you are picturing in your mind. We will also be sending kind thoughts to ourselves and maybe the whole universe.

Before we start, have you ever noticed what a raindrop does when it hits the water? It makes bigger and bigger circles. That is called the "ripple effect." Those circles all came from a common center and the little drop became bigger and bigger, right? In this activity, we will be like raindrops hitting the water as we send well wishes to someone, to ourselves, and to the whole world.

Let's give it a try.

Mindful posture, please.

Take a few natural breaths and maybe a few slower, deeper breaths and allow yourself to be still and calm. You can place your hand on your heart if it makes you feel more heartfelt. Smile.

Close your eyes or gaze down at the floor.

I will begin to say a phrase or a few words of gratitude and will ask you to say these words to yourself. We will pause briefly so you can feel the kindness in your heart and mind.

[Note: You can also ask the students to say the words aloud. We personally love to hear the words out loud and feel it resonates better with the class. You can come up with your own words or phrases; just remember to keep them short and easy to understand. For example, *comforted* or *at ease of heart and mind* may be a little too difficult to interpret or understand for certain age groups, so you would need to discuss what these terms mean if you decide to use them.]

Finally, sometimes there are thoughts we want to send to a person who has been mean to us or a bully that has hurt us, and we want to make things right or kind. We can allow our thoughts to help them and us to bond. Pause and think about this phrase before you begin. Try to be kind to everyone. You never know what someone else is going through.

> *May you be happy.*
> *May you be healthy.*
> *May you feel protected.*

[After these words, invite them to go a little further with their kindness by sending good wishes to themselves.]

> *May I be happy.*
> *May I be healthy.*
> *May I feel protected.*

[If you feel the class still wants to send out more ripples of kindness, continue by reciting together.]

> *May all beings be happy.*
> *May all beings be healthy.*
> *May all beings feel protected.*

[Slowly invite them to open their eyes (or lift their gaze) and smile at each other. Congratulations: you just made someone a little more *happified*!]

Suggested Script: Kind Thoughts 2

This practice is similar to Kind Thoughts 1 but is more generic and uses hand gestures.

The mantra is "Kind thoughts to you, kind thoughts to me, kind thoughts to everybody."

This practice is designed to bring one closer to the meaning of kindness and how it feels in the mind and body. By simply sharing hope, gratitude, or good thoughts, we can bring more joy and happiness to others and ourselves. We recognize that we can all benefit from kindness when we begin to open our hearts to others and to ourselves.

Here are instructions for demonstrating kind thoughts with your body along with your words.

1. Sit up straight and tall.
2. Begin by bringing the backs of both your hands together with your fingers touching your heart or the center of your chest. Say the words "Kind thoughts to you" as you extend your arms out wide in front of you.
3. Bring both hands back together and touch your heart or chest while saying, "Kind thoughts to me."
4. Finally, with your fingertips still on your heart, extend both hands and arms upward over your face and spread out wide while drawing a heart shape in front of you and saying, "Kind thoughts to everybody." Students may express their own movements as they do the practice.

Mindfulness and the Science of Happiness

Positive psychology is the whole field dedicated to the science of happiness and strengths (Carr 2011). Xue (2017) believes that combining mindfulness with positive psychology can make us "super humans" that are more likely to contribute positively to society and to survive. In fact, there is growing evidence that mindfulness can contribute to many of the core positive psychology indices that play a part in making a better society (Ivtzan and Lomas 2016); practicing mindfulness is likely to boost "self-compassion, self-efficacy, meaning, and autonomy" (Ivtzan et al. 2016, 1396). Furthermore, integrating the combination of positive psychology and mindfulness into schools is likely to have many benefits for students, including improving academics, encouraging a growth mindset, and boosting their happiness (Malboeuf-Hurtubise et al. 2017; O'Grady 2015).

Mindfulness fits in nicely with positive psychology because it has the potential to decrease depression and anxiety and increase happiness (Carr 2011). Mindfulness also can lead to greater self-compassion, optimism, and empathy, which all in turn may boost happiness (Carr). Since mindfulness has been recognized for its physical and psychological benefits, it has even been integrated into some positive psychology therapies (Carr). Mindfulness can contribute to resilience (our ability to recuperate after adverse situations), which is very likely to boost our happiness (Bajaj and Pande 2016). In sum, using mindfulness and positive psychology together is a scientific way of making us happier.

SHARE SOME KINDNESS TO CREATE HAPPINESS

Being generous and kind can help you not only survive (Xue 2017) but also be happier. Here are a few ways to share kindness and bring happiness to yourself and others.

- Call someone instead of texting. You just might find how great it is to hear someone's voice, and they might need it too.

- Write a quick, kind note. For example: "Happy Monday! Just wanted to let you know I wish you the best today on your test."

- Start a gratitude journal and write down what you are thankful for when you have a grateful feeling.

- Vow to do one random act of kindness every day.

- STOP and be still at least once a day: stop, take a breath, observe, proceed.

- Try a 30-day challenge with a friend: do something kind every day for one month.

- Share something positive with someone before you go to bed.

- Find your favorite gratitude or happiness quote and post it in your room or home, or share it with your friends and family. Here are two of the author's favorites:

"Let us always meet with a smile, for the smile is the beginning of love." —*Mother Teresa of Calcutta*

"Happiness depends upon ourselves." —*Aristotle*

Gratitude

Gratitude is another key concept studied by positive psychologists. According to Robert Emmons, a renowned gratitude researcher, feeling and expressing gratitude can reap social, physical, and psychological benefits. Socially, gratitude can help people be "more helpful, generous, compassionate, forgiving, and outgoing [and] feel less lonely and isolated" (Emmons, n.d.). Physically, it can improve the immune system, blood pressure, and sleep. Psychologically, it can increase alertness and positive emotions like happiness, optimism, joy, and pleasure. Gratitude also tends to reduce uncomfortable emotions and stress. Expressing it to others also seems to create a positive feedback loop because others are likely to react positively. And the good news is that gratitude can be learned and increased through practice (Emmons) and mindfulness is likely to increase gratitude (Ivtzan et al. 2016).

ACTIVITY

Three Good Things

Writing down or saying out loud three things you are grateful for is a super simple activity, but it sometimes seems hard to do on a daily basis. It is a scientific way to add more happy moments to your life (Carr 2011).

Some use this practice just before bedtime to have a sense of contentment and, hopefully, sweet dreams.

INSTRUCTIONS:

1. Breathe in the good "thing" you noticed, experienced, or felt today.
2. Exhale with "thank you."
3. Repeat with two other things you're grateful for.

Contributor's Personal Reflection

I have been engaging in the Three Good Things practice with a friend for over two years and can honestly say it has made a difference in my mood and overall outlook of each day. Our ground rules are to use one word or a short sentence that we can expand on if we want, or just leave it there. No explanation is needed. The goal is to see the good and stimulate those feel-good hormones in our bodies, even if just for a moment.

Author's Personal Reflection

I have been sharing three things I have been grateful for with a friend for over 10 years. This practice has helped me to slow down and reflect once a day. It has increased the bond I have with my friend, despite the fact that we now live in different countries with a 14-hour time difference. I firmly believe it has increased my appreciation of life and contributed to my happiness and that of my friend.

ACTIVITY

Gratitude Word Cloud

Making a Gratitude Word Cloud is another twist on the Three Good Things activity above. It is a fun and easy way to really get your students interested in and engaged with gratitude by helping them "explore their thoughts . . . and feelings of being grateful" (York, n.d.).

PREPARATION: You can find the Gratitude Word Cloud activity free online (teacherspayteachers.com/Product/Gratitude-Cloud-Activity-3442390).

INSTRUCTIONS:

1. Ask students to write down on a small piece of paper three things they are grateful for (parents, teachers, clothes, warmth, food).
2. You may opt for some ground rules, such as omitting the names of people or pets (to keep their answers anonymous) and discouraging listing games or electronics.

3. Collect the slips of paper and tell them you will share their anonymous results at the next class meeting. At this point, do not reveal *how* you will share the results.

4. Use any word cloud app or online word generator to tally the results for your gratitude cloud. The most frequent words will appear bigger: the bigger the word, the more common the response.

5. Present the cloud on a smartboard or overhead projector and let the students voice what they see to stimulate discussion.

6. Gratitude clouds can be posted on bulletin boards, in parent newsletters, and so on. It is infectious, and students seem to be more joyful and kind to their peers after participating in this activity.

Gratitude Scavenger Hunt

This is a good activity if you need to let the class move around a bit. It works best if students have some time, freedom, and space to roam about. Perhaps work with your physical education teacher to lead this exercise outdoors. Create your own list or modify the list provided in this guidebook as you wish.

There are many things to appreciate and be thankful for within our surroundings and oftentimes right in front of us, yet we rarely notice them in the present moment. If you choose to pause, slow down, and pay attention using all your senses, you just might find a moment that brings a slice of joy, happiness, or peace. Who doesn't want that?

You will find a gratitude scavenger hunt worksheet in the Extra Activities section (see page 76).

Gratitude Box

Gratitude boxes—sometimes called joy jars—are fun to create and have a powerful impact on positivity and compassion. There are so many things to be grateful for, so why not capture them when you feel them?

You can use the box as a daily practice for students to add one good thing or as a container for random, spontaneous entries as students feel something they are grateful for in the moment. The entries can be read aloud or posted on a classroom bulletin board. It is not important to have them sign their name or identify who wrote what; the point is to capture the moment someone felt grateful. For older students, you could allow them to visit and pull from the box when they feel a need for a boost of happiness or distraction from their troubles at hand. Gratitude boxes are a great addition to calming corners in schools as well (see More Ways to Use the Vowels, page 78).

All you need is a box or jar labeled "Gratitude" or something catchy that you and your students agree upon. Have slips of paper next to the box so students can write down their heartfelt moments of happiness or something they are thankful for today. Encourage students to start a gratitude box or jar at home or with friends. It works for all ages.

Be careful—this may be infectious!

Critical Thinking!

- Do a quick review of the Lesson 5 activities and learning principles.
- What does the word *understanding* mean to you? What have you done to be kind to someone today?
- Name three things you are grateful for at this very moment.

Y is for You

Find fun ways to use mindfulness every day

OBJECTIVE

Discover how you can have fun by using mindfulness at school, home, and play.

THE VOWELS OF MINDFULNESS

There are plenty of ways to use mindfulness. You can use it anytime!

Playing with a pet

Walking in nature

Brushing your teeth

Noticing a feeling in the mind and body

Sharing a smile or an act of kindness

"You" can focus and pay attention to your senses a little every day.

Mindfulness can make you become calmer, happier, and more alert.

Y is for You

Paying attention to the present makes your experiences fun,
and might just help with your studies too.
When have you used mindfulness? How did it make you feel?

Introduction

Say that the last vowel is *Y*: You.

Y is for You

Note to Teachers

Explain to the students that there are plenty of ways to use mindfulness. Mindfulness can make you become happier (Carr 2011), calmer, and more alert.

The *Y* is all about what *you* have learned to do, feel, see, and enjoy. And it's about growing in mindfulness: paying attention to things large or small.

This last lesson allows for an open discussion while reinforcing the positive benefits of mindfulness.

You can tell your students, "You can focus and pay attention to your senses a little every day. Paying attention to the present makes your experiences fun and might just help with your studies too."

Encourage them to try mindfulness when they're doing the following:

- Brushing their teeth
- Playing with a pet
- Walking in nature
- Sharing a smile or an act of kindness
- Noticing a feeling in the mind and body
- Eating food

When have you used mindfulness? How did it make you feel? We all need reminders of the importance of being mindful whether at school, home, or play.

Little Green Dots

The purpose of this activity is to remind students to be present and mindful throughout the day. It was inspired by Judy England's Little Green Dots practice (England 2011) as described in an essay written by Saki Santorelli (1996).

This activity is a super simple and fun way to check in with your own awareness of what is happening in the moment. Think about how you can bring more focus and attention to the things you might normally do on autopilot. Find spaces and places where you might need to be reminded to be present and aware.

PREPARATION: Purchase dot stickers online or from your local stationery store.

INSTRUCTIONS:

1. Place about six to eight dots around the classroom or school.
2. Invite students to participate in the activity: "Take a breath each time you see a dot and ask yourself what you are feeling, thinking, and experiencing in that very moment."
3. Then say, "Take another breath and then return to what you were doing in a more mindful way."
4. Give students extra dots to place around their homes (bathroom mirror, refrigerator, bedside, pictures of family or friends, computer or device where they might send text messages) to remind them to pay attention to their immediate surroundings and thoughts or recognize some gratitude.
5. Encourage students to share stickers with their parents and friends to make this activity more interactive.

CAUTION: Use stickers that are easy to remove and do not damage surfaces.

Author's Note

I personally have stickers on my car steering wheel, bicycle helmet, electronic devices, keys, and kitchen utensils, which remind me to take more meaningful breaths and check in with the here and now.

Alternate Activity

Instead of green dots, use gold foil star stickers to remind students that they are stars, especially when they are mindful.

Critical Thinking!

Do a quick review of the Lesson 6 activities and learning principles.

Discuss with the students how they can incorporate mindfulness in their daily lives. Ask them when and where they plan to practice mindfulness.

Questions to prompt more thought or discussion:

- When you are waking up and stepping out of bed, can you notice the temperature of the floor?
- When you are brushing your teeth, can you feel the sensation of the toothbrush or taste the toothpaste?
- When you are eating, can you notice the taste or smell of the food?
- When you are washing your hands, can you feel the temperature of the water, or feel the sensation of soap on your skin?
- When you are walking to school, can you notice the sounds of the traffic or feel the temperature outside?
- Where will you place your green dots or gold stars as a reminder to be mindful?

Extra Activities

ACTIVITY
Marble Roll

Students will connect a link of tubes and roll a marble from one end to the other without dropping it. The purpose of this activity is for students to discover that it takes attention, teamwork, and using all their senses to accomplish their goal.

PREPARATION:

- Cardboard paper towel rolls (one for each student)
- Marbles
- Heavy-duty tape, crayons, or markers

INSTRUCTIONS:

1. Collect paper towel rolls in advance. Students can ask their families to save them and bring them in over time.
2. Students wrap tape around each roll to decorate them and provide more durability. Alternatively, they can decorate each roll with crayons or markers.
3. Explain the activity before you begin. Emphasize the importance of standing still and working together as a team.
4. Students form a straight line and connect all the tubes together, close enough for a seamless line of tubes.
5. The leader or teacher invites the students to take a deep breath and stand tall and still like a mountain.

6. When all are ready, the leader places the marble in the tube, and students at the front of the line gently raise their tubes just enough to start the marble rolling.

7. It is very important for all students to hold tubes end to end or the cycle will break and the marble will drop.

8. The goal is to get the marble from start to finish without it falling out of the tube.

9. You can add more difficulty by reversing the direction of the marble or adding more marbles.

FOLLOW-UP QUESTIONS: What senses did you use in this activity? For example, did you hear the marble? Did you feel the sensation of vibration in your hands as it rolled through your tube? Did you notice any physical sensations in your body as you waited for the marble to reach your tube? Where was your mind during this activity?

These are all excellent questions to ask after each round to increase their awareness and mindfulness. You might repeat the activity so that the students can focus more on the various sensations.

It is hard for students to worry about a test or be distracted when they are engaged in the marble roll activity.

Mindful Bingo

To create the game, you will need to download a bingo card template or use the one above. Add in whatever you decide is appropriate from the mindful activities the students have already learned. This should be a fun activity/game encouraging lots of creativity and laughter!

	M / B	I / I	N / N	D / G	F U L / O
1	Take a deep breath	Name 3 things you are grateful for	Free space	Teach us a stretch or yoga move	Add your own
2	Smile at someone	Free space	Say out loud 3 times fast: rubber baby buggy bumpers	Make an intention for today	Add your own
3	My mind feels, my body feels?	What can you do to calm yourself?	Add your own	Free space	Tell us a pun or joke
4	Share something you like about someone	Free space	Name the last veggie you ate	Add your own	Free space
5	Add your own	What is your mindfulness superpower?	Free space	Compliment yourself	What can we do to help the environment?

Vowels of Mindfulness

Vowels of Mindfulness ● **Can you find all the words?**

```
Z  M  I  N  D  F  U  L  N  E  S  S  I  S  S
N  P  R  A  N  C  H  O  R  W  O  R  D  S  E
S  M  E  L  L  E  M  V  N  C  E  A  S  M  I
P  T  R  Y  R  C  H  E  R  T  A  N  G  I  N
O  E  X  P  E  R  I  E  N  C  E  K  E  L  V
S  I  V  I  L  G  R  A  T  I  T  U  D  E  E
T  O  E  B  A  L  A  N  C  E  O  N  T  T  S
U  B  L  O  X  P  N  A  T  U  U  F  A  H  T
R  S  A  D  I  N  G  N  A  L  C  E  T  O  I
E  E  F  Y  B  B  R  E  A  T  H  E  T  U  G
E  R  O  S  T  A  S  T  E  E  A  L  E  G  A
F  V  C  C  S  A  T  N  S  E  E  I  N  H  T
E  E  U  A  R  W  L  R  I  K  I  N  T  T  E
N  I  S  N  X  A  Y  E  N  I  K  G  I  S  C
D  U  N  D  E  R  S  T  A  N  D  S  O  R  T
T  E  E  R  X  E  T  E  R  D  I  T  N  R  E
```

mindfulness	smell	investigate	kind
gratitude	smile	observe	anchor words
body scan	breathe	understand	thoughts
see	love	posture	feelings
taste	attention	balance	focus
touch	experience	relax	aware

Vowels of Mindfulness • Can you find all the words?

```
Z  M  I  N  D  F  U  L  N  E  S  S  I  S  S
N  P  R  A  N  C  H  O  R  W  O  R  D  S  E
S  M  E  L  L  E  M  V  N  C  E  A  S  M  I
P  T  R  Y  R  C  H  E  R  T  A  N  G  I  N
O  E  X  P  E  R  I  E  N  C  E  K  E  L  V
S  I  V  I  L  G  R  A  T  I  T  U  D  E  E
T  O  E  B  A  L  A  N  C  E  O  N  T  T  S
U  B  L  O  X  P  N  A  T  U  U  F  A  H  T
R  S  A  D  I  N  G  N  A  L  C  E  T  O  I
E  E  F  Y  B  B  R  E  A  T  H  E  T  U  G
E  R  O  S  T  A  S  T  E  E  A  L  E  G  A
F  V  C  C  S  A  T  N  S  E  E  I  N  H  T
E  E  U  A  R  W  L  R  I  K  I  N  G  T  E
N  I  S  N  X  A  Y  E  N  I  K  G  I  S  C
D  U  N  D  E  R  S  T  A  N  D  S  O  R  T
T  E  E  R  X  E  T  E  R  D  I  T  N  R  E
```

mindfulness	smell	investigate	kind
gratitude	smile	observe	anchor words
body scan	breathe	understand	thoughts
see	love	posture	feelings
taste	attention	balance	focus
touch	experience	relax	aware

Gratitude Scavenger Hunt

Your mission, if you choose to accept it, is to find something that brings an awareness to the present and gives you a feeling of gratitude, no matter if it is large or small. Write it down. Why did it make you feel grateful?

1. Find something you enjoy seeing with your eyes.
2. Find something you can hear that you've never heard before.
3. Find something you know someone else would enjoy.
4. Find something that makes you feel safe.
5. Find something that makes you smile or laugh.
6. Find something that is useful to you.
7. Find something that makes you feel calm or relaxed.
8. Find something you enjoy doing with friends.
9. Find something not on the list that you want to note or share that makes you feel grateful.

Spin the Wheel

The wheel serves as an interactive way to gauge your students' understanding of mindfulness.

PREPARATION: Make a spinning wheel that includes a variety of lesson questions.

INSTRUCTIONS: Each student takes a turn spinning the wheel, watches where the arrow stops, and answers the question the arrow points to. Below are some sample questions to get you started.

1. What does an anchor do for a boat?

   ANSWER: *It keeps it steady and keeps it from drifting off. An anchor is commonly used to illustrate how the mind wanders and the anchor can bring it back to the present moment.*

2. Name the five senses. Can you give an example of one of the senses you used today?

   ANSWER: *Sight, sound, smell, taste, touch.*

3. How often does the mind wander, on average?

   ANSWER: *The mind wanders about 50 percent or half of the time each day.*

4. In the *I* vowel (Investigate) lesson, we learned about physical sensations. What is it called when you relax and pay attention to parts of your body like your feet, then ankles, then knees?

   ANSWER: *Body scan or trip around the body.*

5. How can a body scan help you?

   ANSWER: *To help you sleep, calm down, relax, and pause before responding (which is better than reacting without thinking).*

6. Sometimes my thoughts wander and when they do, I can catch them with my hand and then set them free. What is the name for this activity?

   ANSWER: *Firefly Catch.*

7. How can you show gratitude to someone?

   ANSWER: *A smile, a thank-you note, listening with intention (answers will vary).*

8. Now it is your turn to start creating new questions.

More Ways to Use the Vowels

After completing the eight-week curriculum, use the vowels to reinforce learning throughout the year.

1. Develop projects for continued growth and understanding of mindfulness. For older students, consider a project where they teach the concepts of the vowels (Attention, Experience, Investigate, Observe, Understand) to their peers. Each student chooses one activity, develops their own delivery (with teachers' support and guidance), and leads the activity with their classmates. Or divide the class into groups and assign each group a vowel to teach their classmates.

2. Keep it going by empowering students. When students receive feedback, gain confidence, and are comfortable teaching the vowels, they can practice their leadership skills by presenting mindfulness activities to younger students, faculty and staff, or parents as a school-based activity.

3. Be creative with time constraints. The vowels can be taught during lunchtime, after-school programs, and intermissions, or as part of mindfulness clubs or a special event.

4. Bring the vowels into your school's mainstream with poster contests, art projects, drama classes, bulletin boards, health and science fairs, and mindful challenges.

5. Create calming corners in your classroom or school. It can be as simple as a small bookshelf and cozy chair. Read more about calming corners below.

CALMING CORNERS

Perhaps when you were young, you had quiet space—a place to be creative and alone with your imagination. A sacred space to stow your cherished toys, books, puzzles, and collections. A place where you could be yourself.

Calming corners are becoming popular in schools and serve as spaces for quiet, reflective inner thoughts and contemplation. These emerging calming corners are designed for children to visit when they need time to self-regulate from the distractions of everyday life. Students of all ages can calm themselves with some personal reflection, mindful breathing, or just a moment of still time alone.

Mindful corners are spaces set aside to help children sort through problems with intention and clarity, or nurture themselves with positive affirmations, gratitude lists, funny stories, or jokes that help the smile reappear. Young children may want to cuddle a stuffed animal, color, look at a picture book, play with playdough, or write down their feelings, which can help to calm the body and refocus the mind. Does your home or school have one?

Mindful Ethics and Standards

Ethics and standards should be integrated into mindfulness training and curriculum (Monteiro, Compson, and Musten 2017).

There are no all-encompassing official ethical guidelines by a sanctioned organization for teaching mindfulness to children. However, some writers have researched the topic and offer concrete suggestions.

In "Seven Ethical Guidelines for Teaching Mindfulness," Dr. Chris Willard suggests the following: Avoid harm in your teaching; describe your qualifications and experience honestly and plainly; don't work outside of your qualifications alone, or misrepresent your qualifications; and maintain your personal practice (2018). Furthermore, mindfulness teachers should not misrepresent the potential benefits or risks (Monteiro, Compson, and Musten 2017).

Although mindfulness has Buddhist origins, there does not appear to be any conflict in ethically teaching it as a secular practice. That is important because many schools allow only secular teachings. It also is imperative that teachers have a personal practice in order to be authentic.

Another ethical consideration is to be competent in trauma-informed teaching (Schwartz 2019) and, if possible, have school counselors, social workers, or psychologists on hand, since some of the activities could be triggering and traumatic for some students. What's more, mental health professionals are required to adhere to ethical standards that could be relevant for the trauma-informed teaching of mindfulness. For example, the American Psychological Association has ethical standards that psychologists must "strive to benefit those with whom they work and take care to do no harm" (APA 2017, 3).

Because it is beyond the scope of this book to detail all the complexities involved in ethically teaching mindfulness, we highly recommend *Practitioner's Guide to Ethics and Mindfulness-Based Interventions* (Monteiro, Compson, and Musten 2017).

Final Notes

Little Slices of Joy

When I lived in a small military community in base housing, I would often see children playing near my house after school. When they spotted me, their mindfulness teacher, they would stop and do something mindful. Once, I was out jogging and a former student was skateboarding down the street. He was moving along pretty steadily, helmet in hand. As soon as he saw me, he stopped and put on his helmet. As he passed, he said hello and thanked me for teaching him to be mindful. It was a little slice of joy for me. Perhaps he just saw me as an adult, but in my mind, I served as a reminder for him to pay attention to the present moment. After that day, when I would see him and his friends playing in the park, they would always stop whatever they were doing, stand upright, and begin walking slowly and mindfully on the sidewalk. It was a nice connection for us both, and a reminder to pause on occasion and slow things down a bit.

Wishing you all the best in your journey to find your own little slices of joy!

—*Jana York, MS, Mindfulness Educator and Practitioner*

I have also experienced many little slices of joy from my work with mindfulness. When counseling, I often teach my clients mindfulness exercises to help them with emotional regulation, attention, concentration, and relaxation. Once, as a school counselor, I worked with a nine-year-old girl who was referred to me for aggressive behaviors. During our counseling sessions, I taught her how to take calming breaths and then to go through experiencing her five senses.

One day when I entered her classroom looking for another student, I saw her advancing on a boy with her fists clenched and raised. The moment she saw me, her face turned red, she paused, and I could visibly see her take a few breaths that looked more like angry huffs than calming breaths. But that slight pause seemed to be enough: she then slowly approached the boy and led him through finding things to see, hear, smell, touch, and taste in the classroom. Watching this beautiful little slice of joy reminded me that mindfulness is timeless and applicable to all people and all situations.

Be curious about you,

—*Amoneeta Beckstein, PhD, Psychologist*

Resources

Here are two of our favorite authors and books on breathing and other mindfulness activities:

Bergstrom, Christian. 2019. *Ultimate Mindfulness Activity Book: 150 Playful Mindfulness Activities for Kids and Teens (and Grown-Ups Too!)*. Blissful Consulting.

Bergstrom also wrote a helpful article explaining mindfulness and the brain: upfind.me/mindfulness-and-the-brain-how-to-explain-it-to-children.

Willard, Christopher, and Daniel Rechtschaffen. 2019. *Alphabreaths: The ABCs of Mindful Breathing*. Sounds True.

References

Alpart, J. M. 2019. "Effects of Mindfulness Meditation on Parasympathetic Nervous System Measures, Anxiety, Stress and Coping in Adults." ProQuest Dissertation database, Chestnut Hill College.

APA (American Psychological Association). 2006. "Multitasking: Switching Costs." March 20, 2006. Accessed May 12, 2020. https://www.apa.org/research/action/multitask.

APA (American Psychological Association). 2017. "Ethical Principles of Psychologists and Code of Conduct." Accessed July 15, 2020. https://www.apa.org/ethics/code.

APA (American Psychological Association). 2018. "Stress Effects on the Body." American Psychological Association. November 18, 2018. Accessed May 29, 2020. https://www.apa.org/helpcenter/stress-body.

Bajaj, B., and N. Pande. 2016. "Mediating Role of Resilience in the Impact of Mindfulness on Life Satisfaction and Affect as Indices of Subjective Well-Being." *Personality and Individual Differences* 93: 63–67. https://doi.org/10.1016/j.paid.2015.09.005.

Bauer, C. C. C., C. Caballero, E. Scherer, M. R. West, M. D. Mrazek, D. T. Phillips, S. Whitfield-Gabrieli, and J. D. E. Gabrieli. 2019. "Mindfulness Training Reduces Stress and Amygdala Reactivity to Fearful Faces in Middle-School Children." *Behavioral Neuroscience* 133 (6): 569–585. https://doi.org/10.1037/bne0000337.

Blair, C. 2017. "Educating Executive Function." *Wiley Interdisciplinary Reviews. Cognitive Science* 8 (1–2): 10.1002/wcs.1403. https://doi.org/10.1002/wcs.1403.

Bochun, P. 2011. "Mindfulness and Creativity." *Canadian Teacher Magazine.* (November/December 2011). Accessed May 11, 2020. https://www.sterlinghall.com/uploaded/The_Institute/News/Mindfulness_and_Creativity.pdf.

Bonfil, A. 2014. *Cognitive Behavioral Therapy Los Angeles* (blog). June 24, 2014. Accessed July 21, 2020. http://cogbtherapy.com/mindfulness-meditation-blog.

Carr, A. 2011. *Positive Psychology: The Science of Happiness and Human Strengths.* Abingdon, UK: Taylor & Francis.

Davis, M., and P. J. Whalen. 2000. "The Amygdala: Vigilance and Emotion." *Molecular Psychiatry* 6 (1): 13–34. https://doi.org/10.1038/sj.mp.4000812.

Emmons, R. n.d. "Why Gratitude Is Good." *Greater Good Magazine.* Accessed June 27, 2020. https://greatergood.berkeley.edu/article/item/why_gratitude_is_good.

England, J. 2011. "All You've Got to Do Is Pay Attention to the Green Dots." *Albany Times Union Holistic Health.* May 23, 2011. Accessed May 29, 2020. http://mystorylives.blogspot.com/2011/05/all-youve-got-to-do-is-pay-attention-to.html.

Frankl, V. E. 1946. *Man's Search for Meaning.* New York: Pocket Books.

Fuster, J. M. 2008. *The Prefrontal Cortex.* 4th ed. Burlington, MA: Academic Press.

Giovannini, M., E. Verduci, S. Scaglioni, E. Salvatici, M. Bonza, E. Riva, and C. Agostoni. 2008. "Breakfast: A Good Habit, Not a Repetitive Custom." *Journal of International Medical Research* 36 (4): 613–624. https://doi.org/10.1177/147323000803600401.

Goldstein, E. 2012. *The Now Effect: How a Mindful Moment Can Change the Rest of Your Life.* New York: Atria Books / Simon & Schuster.

Hansen, M. M., R. Jones, and K. Tocchini. 2017. "Shinrin-Yoku (Forest Bathing) and Nature Therapy: A State-of-the-Art Review." *International Journal of Environmental Research and Public Health* 14 (8): 851. https://doi.org/10.3390/ijerph14080851.

Hanson, R. 2018. "Take in the Good." *Just One Thing* (newsletter). July 29, 2018. Accessed May 29, 2020. https://www.rickhanson.net/take-in-the-good/.

Hölzel, B. K., J. Carmody, K. C. Evans, E. A. Hoge, J. A. Dusek, L. Morgan, and S. W. Lazar. 2009. "Stress Reduction Correlates with Structural Changes in the Amygdala." *Social Cognitive and Affective Neuroscience* 5 (1): 11–17. https://doi.org/10.1093/scan/nsp034.

Hölzel, B. K., J. Carmody, M. Vangel, C. Congleton, S. M. Yerramsetti, T. Gard, and S. W. Lazar. 2011. "Mindfulness Practice Leads to Increases in Regional Brain Gray Matter Density." *Psychiatry Research: Neuroimaging* 191 (1): 36–43. https://doi.org/10.1016/j.pscychresns.2010.08.006.

Hopkins, C. 2016. *Breathing Anchor* (video). July 17, 2016. Accessed May 11, 2020. https://www.youtube.com/watch?v=yZYUJafIKOs.

Hoyland, A., L. Dye, and C. L. Lawton. 2009. "A Systematic Review of the Effect of Breakfast on the Cognitive Performance of Children and Adolescents. *Nutrition Research Reviews* 22 (2): 220–243. https://doi.org/10.1017/s0954422409990175.

Hyman, I. E. 2014. "The Dangers of Going on Autopilot." April 28, 2014. Accessed May 11, 2020. https://www.psychologytoday.com/us/blog/mental-mishaps/201404/the-dangers-going-autopilot.

Ideas2earnmore. 2011. *Kung Fu Panda: Today Is a Gift* (video). Accessed May 29, 2020. https://www.youtube.com/watch?v=H7BwWNMFJwE.

Ivtzan, I., and T. Lomas, eds. 2016. *Mindfulness in Positive Psychology: The Science of Meditation and Wellbeing.* London: Routledge/Taylor & Francis Group.

Ivtzan, I., T. Young, J. Martman, A. Jeffrey, T. Lomas, R. Hart, and F. J. Eiroa-Orosa. 2016. "Integrating Mindfulness into Positive Psychology: A Randomised Controlled Trial of an Online Positive Mindfulness Program." *Mindfulness* 7 (6): 1396–1407. https://doi.org/10.1007/s12671-016-0581-1.

Kabat-Zinn, J. 1994. *Wherever You Go, There You Are: Mindfulness Meditation in Everyday Life.* New York: Hyperion.

Kabat-Zinn, J. 2013. *Full Catastrophe Living: Using the Wisdom of Your Body and Mind to Face Stress, Pain, and Illness.* New York: Bantam Books / Random House.

Kabat-Zinn, J. 2016. *Mindfulness for Beginners: Reclaiming the Present Moment—and Your Life.* Louisville, CO: Sounds True.

Kaiser Greenland, Susan. 2016. *Mindful Games: Sharing Mindfulness and Meditation with Children, Teens, and Families.* Boulder, CO: Shambhala Publications.

Klechaya, R., and G. Glasson. 2017. "Mindfulness and Place-Based Education in Buddhist-Oriented Schools in Thailand." In *Weaving Complementary Knowledge Systems and Mindfulness to Educate a Literate Citizenry for Sustainable and Healthy Lives*, edited by M. Powietrzynska and K. Tobin. https://doi.org/10.1007/978-94-6351-182-7_11.

Koeppen, A. S. 1974. "Relaxation Training for Children." *Elementary School Guidance & Counseling* 9 (1): 14–21.

Kubu, C., and A. Machado. 2017. "Why Multitasking Doesn't Work." *Health Essentials* (blog), Cleveland Clinic. Accessed May 12, 2020. https://health.clevelandclinic.org/science -clear-multitasking-doesnt-work/.

Leland, M. 2015. "Mindfulness and Student Success." *Journal of Adult Education* 44 (1): 19–24.

Mackereth, P. A., and L. T. Tomlinson. 2010. "Progressive Muscle Relaxation: A Remarkable Tool for Therapists and Patients. In *Integrative Hypnotherapy: Complementary Approaches in Clinical Care*, edited by Anne Cawthorn and Peter A. Mackereth. N.p.: Churchill Livingstone.

Malboeuf-Hurtubise, C., G. Taylor, D. Lefrançois, I. Essopos, and E. Lacourse. 2017. "The Impact of a Mindfulness-Based Intervention on Happiness: A Reflection on the Relevance of Integrating a Positive Psychology Framework within Mindfulness Research in Youth." *International Journal of Applied Positive Psychology* 2 (1–3): 23–37. https://doi .org/10.1007/s41042-017-0010-2.

McCorry L. K. 2007. "Physiology of the Autonomic Nervous System." *American Journal of Pharmaceutical Education* 71 (4): 78. https://www.ncbi.nlm.nih.gov/pmc/articles/PMC1959222/.

Meiklejohn, J., C. Phillips, M. L. Freedman, M. L. Griffin, G. Biegel, A. Roach, J. Frank, C. Burke, L. Pinger, G. Soloway, R. Isberg, E. Sibinga, L. Grossman, and A. Saltzman. 2012. "Integrating Mindfulness Training into K-12 Education: Fostering the Resilience of Teachers and Students." *Mindfulness* 3 (4): 291–307. https://psycnet.apa.org/doi/10.1007 /s12671-012-0094-5.

Mindful Schools 2010–2019. Accessed at https://www.mindfulschools.org.

Mindful Schools. 2014. *Mindfulness Curriculum: Kindergarten–5th Grades*. Emeryville, CA: Mindful Schools.

Mindfulness in Schools Project (MiSP). 2016. *Playing Attention* (video). Accessed July 19, 2020. https://www.youtube.com/watch?v=LgXZW6Xqokw

Monteiro, L., J. F. Compson, and F. Musten, eds. 2017. *Practitioner's Guide to Ethics and Mindfulness-Based Interventions*. N.p.: Springer Nature.

Moore, C. 2019. "What Is the Negativity Bias and How Can It Be Overcome?" PositivePsy-chology.com. December 30, 2019. Accessed May 12, 2020. https://positivepsychology .com/3-steps-negativity-bias/.

Murphy, M. J., L. C. Mermelstein, K. M. Edwards, and C. A. Gidycz. 2012. "The Benefits of Dispositional Mindfulness in Physical Health: A Longitudinal Study of Female College Students." *Journal of American College Health* 60 (5): 341–348. https://doi.org/10.1080/ 07448481.2011.629260.

Napoli, M., P. R. Krech, and L. C. Holley. 2005. "Mindfulness Training for Elementary School Students." *Journal of Applied School Psychology* 21 (1): 99–125. https://stressbeaters .com/wp-content/uploads/2011/08/WAPP_A_428098_O_merged.pdf.

National Geographic. 2018. "Fireflies." September 24, 2018. Accessed May 29, 2020. https:// www.nationalgeographic.com/animals/invertebrates/group/fireflies/.

O'Grady, P. 2015. "Positive Psychology of Mindfulness." July 27, 2015. Accessed June 27, 2020. https://www.psychologytoday.com/intl/blog/positive-psychology-in-the-classroom /201507/positive-psychology-mindfulness.

O'Sullivan, T. A., M. Robinson, G. E. Kendall, M. Miller, P. Jacoby, S. R. Silburn, and W. H. Oddy. 2009. "A Good-Quality Breakfast Is Associated with Better Mental Health in Adolescence." *Public Health Nutrition* 12 (2): 249–258. https://doi.org/10.1017/s1368980008003935.

Park, B. J., Y. Tsunetsugu, T. Kasetani, T. Kagawa, and Y. Miyazaki. 2009. "The Physiological Effects of *Shinrin-Yoku* (Taking in the Forest Atmosphere or Forest Bathing): Evidence from Field Experiments in 24 Forests across Japan." *Environmental Health and Preventive Medicine* 15 (1): 18–26. https://doi.org/10.1007/s12199-009-0086-9.

Portia, N. 1993. *There's a Hole in My Sidewalk: The Romance of Self-Discovery.* Hillsboro, OR: Beyond Words Publishing.

Ressler, K. J. 2010. "Amygdala Activity, Fear, and Anxiety: Modulation by Stress." *Biological Psychiatry* 67 (12): 1117–1119. https://doi.org/10.1016/j.biopsych.2010.04.027.

Rideout, V., and M. B. Robb. 2019. "The Common Sense Census: Media Use by Tweens and Teens, 2019." San Francisco, CA: Common Sense Media. Accessed May 13, 2020. https://www.commonsensemedia.org/sites/default/files/uploads/research/2019-census-8-to-18-full-report-updated.pdf.

Robson, D. A., M. S. Allen, and S. J. Howard. 2020. "Self-Regulation in Childhood as a Predictor of Future Outcomes: A Meta-Analytic Review." *Psychological Bulletin* 146 (4): 324–354.

Santorelli, S. 1996. "Mindfulness and Mastery in the Workplace: 21 Ways to Reduce Stress During the Workday." In *Engaged Buddhist Reader: Ten Years of Engaged Buddhist Publishing*, edited by Arnold Kotler. Berkeley: Parallax Press.

Schwartz, K. 2019. "Why Mindfulness and Trauma-Informed Teaching Don't Always Go Together." KQED. January 27, 2019. Accessed May 12, 2020. https://www.kqed.org/mindshift/52881/why-mindfulness-and-trauma-informed-teaching-dont-always-go-together.

Sessa, S. A. 2007. "Meditation, Breath Work, and Focus Training for Teachers and Students: The Five Minutes a Day That Can Really Make a Difference." *Journal of College Teaching & Learning* 4 (10). https://doi.org/10.19030/tlc.v4i10.1536.

Thierry, K. L., H. L. Bryant, S. S. Nobles, and K. S. Norris. 2016. "Two-Year Impact of a Mindfulness-Based Program on Preschoolers' Self-Regulation and Academic Performance." *Early Education and Development* 27 (6): 805–821. https://doi.org/10.1080/10409289.2016.1141616.

UWSHS (University of Windsor Student Health Services). 2018. "Relax Your Stress Triangle." Accessed May 12, 2020. http://www.uwindsor.ca/studenthealthservices/527/relax-your-stress-triangle.

Viafora, D. P., S. G. Mathiesen, and S. J. Unsworth. 2014. "Teaching Mindfulness to Middle School Students and Homeless Youth in School Classrooms." *Journal of Child and Family Studies* 24 (5): 1179–1191. https://doi.org/10.1007/s10826-014-9926-3.

Weare, K. 2012. "Evidence for the Impact of Mindfulness on Children and Young People." The Mindfulness in Schools Project (MiSP) / University of Exeter Mood Disorders Centre. April 2012.

Willard, C. 2018. "Seven Ethical Guidelines for Teaching Mindfulness." Drchristopherwillard.com. May 10, 2018. https://www.susankaisergreenland.com/blog/2018/5/8/seven-ethical-guidelines-for-teaching-mindfulness-to-children-and-families-by-chris-willard.

Willard, C., and A. J. Nance. 2018. "A Mindful Kids Practice: The Breath Ball." May 25, 2018. Accessed May 11, 2020. https://www.mindful.org/a-mindful-kids-practice-the-breath-ball/.

Wyzowl. n.d. "The Shortening Human Attention Span." Infographic. Accessed May 29, 2020. https://www.wyzowl.com/human-attention-span/.

Xue, J. 2017. "How Mixing Mindfulness with Positive Psychology Makes You a 'Super Human.'" September 6, 2017. Accessed June 27, 2020. https://thriveglobal.com/stories/how-mixing -mindfulness-with-positive-psychology-makes-you-a-super-human/.

Yaribeygi, H., Y. Panahi, H. Sahraei, T. P. Johnston, and A. Sahebkar. 2017. "The Impact of Stress on Body Function: A Review." *EXCLI Journal* 16: 1057–1072. https://doi.org/10.17179 /excli2017-480.

Yeo, A. 2016. "The Story of Two Wolves." Urban Balance. February 24, 2016. Accessed May 29, 2020. https://urbanbalance.com/the-story-of-two-wolves/.

York, J. n.d. "Gratitude Cloud Activity." Teachers Pay Teachers. Accessed May 12, 2020. https:// www.teacherspayteachers.com/Product/Gratitude-Cloud-Activity-3442390.

Zelazo, P. D., and K. E. Lyons. 2012. "The Potential Benefits of Mindfulness Training in Early Childhood: A Developmental Social Cognitive Neuroscience Perspective." *Child Development Perspectives* 6 (2): 154–160. https://doi.org/10.1111/j.1750-8606.2012.00241.x.

Index

"Mindfulness is paying attention on purpose in the present moment with kindness and curiosity."

JON KABAT-ZINN

FOCUS ON YOUR BREATH

ANCHOR WORDS
CALM RELAX BREATHE

MINDFUL BODIES

ACTIVITY: Mindful bodies, awareness of breathing, anchor words. Practice mindful breathing for one minute.

A is for Attention

Focus or concentrate on what is happening now. While it is important to pay attention to many things, you can also use mindfulness with a spirit of curiosity and a sense of wonderment.

The average web page visit lasts less than a minute and users often leave pages in just 10–20 seconds.

Typical office workers check their email inbox 30 times every hour.

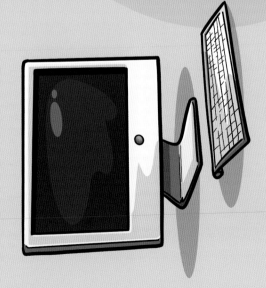

On the average web page, users will read at most 28% of the words during a normal visit; 20% is more likely.

Attention? We are so easily distracted!

The average user picks up their phone more than 1,500 times a week, using up an average of 3 hours, 16 minutes a day.

According to research, our average attention span has greatly decreased in just 15 years.

ATTENTION SPAN · 12 SECONDS IN 2000 · 8 SECONDS IN 2015

HUMANS

Scientists suggest that people now have shorter attention spans than goldfish.

A GOLDFISH ATTENTION SPAN IS ONLY 9 SECONDS LONG

Attention? People are so forgetful!

7% of people forget their own birthday from time to time.

25% of teenagers forget major details of their close friends and relatives.

39% of Americans will forget one basic piece of information or lose one everyday item this week!

THE VOWELS OF MINDFULNESS

"Yesterday is history, tomorrow is a mystery, today is a gift. That's why it is called the present."

KUNG FU PANDA

We often run on autopilot, which means we do things without even thinking about them.

Being on autopilot can lead to mistakes or you may miss a very enjoyable moment with friends.

Experience and enjoy the present moment using all of your senses.

SEE .... **HEAR** .... **SMELL** .... **TOUCH** .... **TASTE**

E is for Experience

Experience the present moment: Take time to walk slowly in nature. Listen to the birds and the sounds around you. Touch the ground, and notice if it is hot or cold, rough or smooth. Finally, take a mindful mouthful, and use all your senses to enjoy fresh food and cake!

Look closely at the leaves that have fallen from the trees.

ACTIVITY: Mindful mouthful; mindful walking in nature; mindful listening; seeing; etc.

Try the body scan at night

to help you calm down or sleep.

Do you ever feel tense or notice tight muscles when you are annoyed?

If you notice these sensations, you can investigate them further.

See if you can notice what your body feels like right now.

Does your heart beat fast or stomach feel squishy before you take a test?

How can you make your body calm and relaxed?

I is for Investigate

Are there any physical sensations that you can feel right now? We call this the "physical sensations" in the body. What does the physical body feel like when you are nervous, excited, tired, happy, or having a strong emotion?

ACTIVITY: Trip around the body/body scan, slow-motion movement, balance—Tree Posture, squeeze and relax.

THE VOWELS OF MINDFULNESS

THOUGHTS

The strong ones (negative thoughts) stick in our mind more than positive thoughts.

THOUGHTS

Our minds wander about 50% of the time

THOUGHTS

If you observe your thoughts, you can notice which ones to keep and which ones to let pass by.

THOUGHTS

O is for Observe

Observe your thoughts and feelings (emotions) like clouds passing in the sky.

THE VOWELS OF MINDFULNESS

THOUGHTS

Imagine your sibling keeps bothering you, and you want them to stop. Instead of reacting by yelling at them, take a breath, and allow some space so you won't say something you might regret.

Hold your index finger close to the second finger. Use mindfulness and open the two fingers to make space. You just created the peace sign.

THOUGHTS

Here is another idea to help you think about mindfulness. I hope it can work for you to be mindful of your responses in difficult situations.

S.T.O.P. = Stop, Take a breath, Observe your thought, Proceed.

ACTIVITY: Firefly catch, finger breathing, count to 10—count each breath for one minute.

THE VOWELS OF MINDFULNESS

U is for Understand

You can be generous by just sharing a smile!

You can be understanding just by listening to someone.

If you make someone happy, it makes you feel good too.

Try being kind and caring on the playground.

Be kind to yourself and to others and show them gratitude.

ACTIVITY: Gratitude jar, 3 good things, kindness practice

THE VOWELS OF MINDFULNESS

There are plenty of ways to use mindfulness. You can use it anytime!

Sharing a smile or an act of kindness

Brushing your teeth

Walking in nature

Playing with a pet

Noticing a feeling in the mind and body

Mindfulness can make you become calmer, happier, and more alert.

"You" can focus and pay attention to your senses a little every day.

Y is for You

Paying attention to the present makes your experiences fun, and might just help with your studies too.

When have you used mindfulness? How did it make you feel?

About the Authors

Amoneeta Beckstein, PhD, is a multicultural, positive psychologist and an ethical influencer who advocates for positive mental health and social justice. He was the counseling center director and a psychology faculty member at Webster University Thailand from 2017–2021. He is currently a psychology professor at Fort Lewis College in Durango, Colorado, and adjunct faculty and clinical supervisor in the counseling psychology graduate program at Assumption University of Thailand. His doctoral degree is from Arizona State University. Dr. Amoneeta often integrates mindfulness into his teaching, therapy, and service and is particularly interested in how mindfulness can contribute to people's happiness and inner peace and to society's growth, resilience, and life enhancement.

Jana York, MS, has been a children's mindfulness educator and mindfulness practitioner for more than a decade. She has conducted research and written on mindfulness. York is the author of *U Is for Understanding: Claire's Journey toward Mindfulness*, a chapter book designed to introduce mindfulness and social-emotional learning to children. The activities are based on her training and teaching to adults and students in various cultures around the globe. Her passion is teaching children how to reduce anxiety and self-regulate while being in the present moment. She is an avid practitioner of mindfulness in her personal life.

CONTACT INFORMATION

Dr. Amoneeta Beckstein
Email: amoneeta@asu.edu

Ms. Jana York
Email: janayork.mindful@gmail.com